Caring For Aging Parents Without Losing Your Mind!

Shannon West

Copyright © 2025 Transformative Legacy Consulting and Coaching LLC, Shannon West. All rights reserved.

This is a work of creative nonfiction. While some names and identifying details may have been changed to protect privacy, the stories, lessons, and reflections are drawn from real experiences and genuine moments in the caregiving journey. No part of this publication may be reproduced, distributed, or transmitted in any form or by any means, including photocopying, recording, or electronic methods, without the prior written permission of the author, except for brief quotations used in reviews, articles, or noncommercial references permitted by copyright law. For permission requests, contact the author at: ShannonWestAuthor.com

Limit of Liability: The advice and strategies contained herein may not be suitable for every situation. This work is sold with the understanding that this author is not engaged in rendering medical, legal, or other professional advice or services. If professional assistance is required, the services of a competent professional in the field of need should be sought. The author shall not be liable for damages arising herefrom. The fact that an individual, organization, or website is referred to in this work as a citation and/or a potential source of further information does not mean that the author endorses the information the individual, organization, or website may provide or recommendations they/it make. Further, the reader should be aware that websites listed in this work may have changed or disappeared between when this work was written and when it is read.

Edited by Mozelle Jordan

Cover design by Kelly Carter

Printed in the United States of America

First Edition: 2026

Paperback ISBN: 979-8-9932301-0-8

eBook ISBN: 979-8-9932301-1-5

For the "up-and-coming" caregivers of their aging parents, this book is for all of you trying courageously hard to show up and return the favor with grace, caffeine, and a little levity.

To my children, this book is a guide for you when I undoubtedly pluck at your nerves as I try to age resiliently. Now listen, don't say you didn't get a manual! So, take notes and remember, I love you always!

> I've learned that people will forget what you said, people will forget what you did, but people will never forget how you made them feel.
>
> — Maya Angelou

Contents

Prologue	1
INTRODUCTION	7

CHAPTER 1
Hustle to Shuffle: The Aging Shift	15
The "I'm Fine" Era: Where Everything Clearly is Not Fine	27
Good Intentions and a Tough Crowd	30
When the Shift Hits the Fan	33

CHAPTER 2
Respecting Who They Were While Loving Who They're Becoming	47
Caring for the Complicated	58
Celebrating Memories and Creating New Ones	66

CHAPTER 3
Advocacy with HIPAA: The Doc Blocker	71
Now Taking the Mic: Advocating Loudly, Proudly, and with a Giant Binder	76
Pills, Drills, and Calendar Thrills	83

CHAPTER 4
Namaste…Over There: Accepting Imperfection	87
It's Not Selfish, It's Survival. Now Hand Me the Moisturizer!	90
Hustling, Healing, and Hoping for the Best	93

Acknowledgments	96
Resource Roundup	98
About the Author	101

> There have been inner stumbles that challenged my spirit, dark nights when everything felt heavier than I could carry, and yes, there have been full-blown tantrums, mostly mine.

Prologue
• • •

There have been times in my life when I dreamed of being a stay-at-home mom and wife, running a household full-time with a sense of purpose and pride. Those thoughts were usually, and pretty quickly, tempered after a few practice runs, when reality swooped in far louder than the daydream. But even though I accepted that staying at home full-time was not for me, it made me appreciate those who not only made it happen but embraced the exceptional level of endurance that staying at home with your children requires.

If you've never been a part of a dynamic in which you run the home full-time, you may not realize exactly what it requires you to be—the event planner, the short-order cook, the complaint department, and the conflict resolution center. Managing endless lists, being the sole member of a hazmat crew, wrangling school demands, orchestrating extracurricular expectations, and scheduling medical appointments are just the beginning. There's no HR department to lodge a grievance with, no performance reviews that end in raises or promotions, and certainly no days when you get to call in "sick" and "tired." Your kid's favorites become your favorites because even though you're home all day, you rarely get to indulge in the things you enjoy. For example, that sleek playlist of '90s R&B you've been curating for car rides is replaced with an endless barrage of repetitive children's sing-song music. Limited adult interaction becomes the norm, and the daily grind often feels like a loop you can't escape.

Hard pass: I prefer my chaos optional, not on an endless subscription plan. My hat goes off to all stay-at-home parents.

As you might expect, I chose, and still choose, to work full time outside of the home alongside my husband, carefully picking out a great daycare provider for our kids just down the road. Leaving the house for work isn't an escape; it's a recalibration. It's where I can sip my coffee without interruption and complete a sentence without someone yelling my name from another room. By the time I return, I'm slightly more human and ready to jump back into the whirlwind, knowing that tomorrow, I get another breather. In removing the mental pressure that would be caused by one of us staying home, taking on all of those required responsibilities, both of us are able to feel more present when we are home and engaged in the tasks that need our attention. This includes raising our youngest child, training a very stubborn puppy, guiding our two oldest children, and looking after our aging parents, who need more from us as the days slip by.

Now, don't get me wrong—even with the reprieve that working outside the home provides, the demands waiting for me at home don't magically shrink. The laundry still multiples like it's on a secret mission, the fridge is always hungry for more, and the needs of our aging parents don't pause just because I've had a productive day elsewhere. I love my family, I love my parents, and I even love the privilege of being able to show up for them, but love doesn't erase exhaustion. Caring for an aging parent is a wholly different kind of demand, one that tugs at both your time and your heart in ways nothing else does.

 "To care for those that once cared for us is the highest honor."[1]

— Tia Walker

Some days, the struggle of juggling this level of life, specifically when it comes to our parents, is arduously real. As an adult child, I never imagined my parents would need my care, thus redefining the parent–child role. So, after having kids and then understanding that aging parents *do* require help, I realized just how much caregiving had become a central part of my day-to-day. Even when I'm not in physical hands-on caregiving mode, the emotional worry for their well-being just doesn't go away. As a new parent, I had constant anxiety, wondering if my child was making it through daycare okay after I left for work; caring for aging parents presents similar, paralleled uneasiness. The only difference is that I feel this when I'm at work *and* at home.

---

1. Tia Walker, *The Inspired Caregiver: Finding Joy While Caring for Those You Love.* Goodreads.com/quotes/888458-to-care-for-those-who-once-cared-for-us-is

There have been inner stumbles that challenged my spirit, dark nights when everything felt heavier than I could carry, and yes, there have been full-blown tantrums, mostly mine.

Somehow, though, even in the thick of it, there is always a light that finds a way to wriggle through in the form of an exhale, an uncontrollable laugh, or a realization that things could be worse. Each worrisome moment, every emotional crack, every celebratory win, is somehow held together by a love that refuses to break, a grace I'm still learning to give, and a resilience I never saw coming.

> ... the parent-child role reversal transition can be just as frighteningly overwhelming as it is enlightening.

Introduction
. . .

I HAVE THIS REOCCURRING MEMORY OF MY EIGHT-YEAR-OLD SELF, at one of our backyard barbecues on a hot summer day. There were people everywhere, food was on the grill, and tables were filled with everything from salads, to watermelon, to corn on the cob. Kids, including myself, played yard games, while parents exchanged banter, their jokes ringing in the air. And as kids ate popsicles every 15 minutes and binged on sodas in between, parents could be found with a cigarette or Budweiser or some other drink in hand. Then, when the oppressive heat became unbearable, we sought refuge in the cool spray of the water hose, extending our playtime until the stars emerged.

My parents and their friends were stylish, dancing around, laughing, and having a good time, and as I ran around the yard, there were brief moments of pause when I stopped and smiled at all of them. I remember music, amazing music, filling the air, like—"All I Do" by Stevie Wonder, "Brick House" by the Commodores, "I Need Your Lovin'" by Teena Marie. That late '70s and early '80s music was expressive, unapologetic, and a complete vibe. Now, I mostly smile looking back at how cool and smooth they all looked. It never occurred to me that one day, life wouldn't be like that.

So many of our memories are those snippets of minutiae from our youth, when we had no clue there would be an aging decline, or at least the impact of it. Before their gray hairs and medication regimens, they were the ones who danced in the kitchen, let you stay up just past bedtime, sang out of tune during car rides, and often made life feel like a carefree Saturday morning.

Do you recall the first time you realized your parents were aging? Maybe it was the confounding reaction when you noticed that your parent's "get up and go" was happening a little slower. Or when you realized they were uncomfortable driving at night, swaying a bit when they walked, or beginning to put everything off for another day. We should have known this was coming, right? Except, how could we when our parents were those invincible beings who somehow managed to host backyard barbecues, worked 10- to 12-hour shifts, kept a buttered-up gloss on the Buick, handled a salesman like a champ, managed a household, while mastering—or trying to master—raising us. This is partially why the parent–child role reversal transition can be just as frighteningly overwhelming as it is enlightening.

I've spoken to many adult children also caring for their aging parents, and it's amazing how often our journeys echo one another. It's a shift that can leave you feeling discomposed and, at times, nearly submerged as you try to navigate this pool of change with only one arm floaty on. If you're a bit like me, you may be grieving who they once were while loving who they have become. When this struggle surfaces, I often try to remain within the mindset of balance and perspective. Yes, we're helping our parents along the aging roadmap, and it's hard, but the rebalance comes from remembering that countless others would trade places with us in a heartbeat just to have more time with the parent they've already lost. Keeping this balance and perspective is what realigns my exasperation and centers my soul with space to embrace the bigger picture. However, please understand, this mindset shift does take practice and patience.

There will be those moments when you notice there's a problem and you're not quite ready to confront the uncomfortable. The result, in the meantime, is keeping the ever changing "it" to yourself. Can you recall the comic books where every thought and verbal exchange was in the form of a bubble above the character's head? These bubbles gave you clear insight into what they were thinking before they said it out loud. Throughout the evolution of this new normal, becoming my parent's caregiver, I've had "thought bubble above the head" situations in which I had to learn (sometimes the hard way) to ignite my ultra-adulting filter to successfully avoid sharing my thoughts until I was emotionally ready. Such as the initial thought of, "I'm frustrated and embarrassed. How do I respond to this? I don't want to hurt her feelings by mentioning that she's repeated the story." Not being fully prepared to respond in a way that enhances the parent–child bond could exasperate aging challenges, making it incredibly difficult to cope with the changes.

The truth is, facing the myriad of parent–child role reversal difficulties demands confronting uncomfortable realities, not glossing over them with superficial optimism, which may be easier to do. For example, when your parent repeats the same story during dinner three times, laughing each time like it's brand new, you aren't doing anything but telling yourself, "At least they're still laughing." But deep down, you know the repetition is getting worse, and saying it out loud only makes it real. The tougher challenge is addressing the repetitiveness. You might try, "That story always makes you smile, and I love seeing that. You've shared it a couple of times tonight, so it's clearly one of the greats! We should start writing down some of your favorites in a book together. That way, we can keep track of all the gems you've shared." Reframing the repetition as a collaborative project rooted in legacy and storytelling allows you to not only document patterns for future medical insight, it also deepens your connection while preserving their dignity. So, perhaps it helps to lean less into the "superficial," instead gaining comfort responding with tact, love, and diplomacy.

It was in mastering this skill that I was able to find more clarity in what my role as caregiver was meant to be, as well as managing my own emotions and expectations in the process. And because I have found so much success in being able to embrace my new role due to this practice, as well as many others, I now want to share them with you, in the hopes that you can find a little bit of peace and relief with them too.

In *Caring for Aging Parents Without Losing Your Mind!* you will read about frustrations, resolutions, and how to get to a point that allows you to feel the levity with enough grace to allow an exhale. I'll also tackle topics such as having tough conversations, the speed bumps of healthcare, and the crazy (and often hilarious) realities of managing the needs of someone who used to wipe—and sometimes whoop—your butt. I'll also share strategies for self-care, with an emphasis on the importance of setting boundaries, because saying "no" (politely, of course) is a crucial survival skill to help you preserve your well-being and your relationships. And let's be honest, you're no good to anyone if your mindset is zapped.

Here's my disclaimer: I'm not a medical professional, nor do I proclaim to be an expert of any kind. This book is a collection of my experiences and of those around me who've offered support, advice, guidance, and resources to their aging parents.

If you are trying to walk alongside a parent going through their aging process and have a specific interest, prioritize taking on the chapter in this book that calls to where you are in the caregiving journey. And if you're here to get the whole big picture, immerse yourself in it all at once, starting from the very beginning. Whichever path you choose, it's about finding *your* balance and perspective, preserving family relationships, and yes, even trying to find moments of levity amidst the upheaval.

> ...so the wisdom lies in discerning which hills are worth dying on.

One
. . .

Hustle To Shuffle: The Aging Shift

PAYING METICULOUS ATTENTION TO SUBTLE SHIFTS IN BEHAVIOR related to aging is crucial, as the early warning signals that they need assistance might be cleverly concealed beneath a veneer of self-reliance, a stubborn refusal to acknowledge limitations, or even seemingly trivial neglect (a collection of expired condiments when this was something they avidly kept up with in previous years). So, be observant, and be prepared to keep track of any change in their behavior or habits by listing them in a date-driven journal, or a similar tool, so you can measure if the changes are worsening and how quickly.

Offering support to parents going through latter stages of aging, roughly in their 70s, is interesting and filled with many double-take inner questioning experiences. One moment, our parents are up and about, taking care of business (and all in ours) with ease; then slowly, you begin to see glitches in the norm. Consider a car that's seen better days—you know, the one that used to start up with the smoothest purr you've ever heard, but now it backfires with a subtle shimmy long before it eventually clonks out and needs additional support to get safely back on the road. Maybe there were some signs, like taking multiple turns of the ignition before it starts, or a backfiring sputter before taking off, but you tell yourself these changes are normal, and you don't think much of it. That is, until your car can no longer get you from point A to point B, and you're forced to face the facts: your car needs attention. I see aging kind of like that. There are "double-take" situations that might seem insignificant at first, but they're telling you something important—things will get worse if you don't address the small things now.

As I noted above in some of my examples, these early warning signs are rarely dramatic medical emergencies like a sudden fall rendering injury, or complete memory lapses. Those are the "check engine" lights, in your face emergencies. What I'm referring to are the little things; if you don't maintain a keen eye and open mind to their aging, the subtle shifts will stack up and seem as if they came out of nowhere. For example, the mail doesn't get checked for a week, or the desire to handle the nuances of personal affairs declines. Or they make seasonally confused fashion choices, and they justify wearing a parka in 80-degree weather because "it's brisk in the shade." It's subtle clues and warning signs that catch us off guard, and we might find ourselves rationalizing or denying the signs.

It can be difficult to know when to bring up a new behavior to your parent, but if you remember that we as the caregivers to our parents are aging as well, you may see that this comes with an opportunity to embrace the beauty of increased wisdom and a clearer focus on what the small stuff truly is.

Take this brief story: a daughter notices her mother's shirt is on inside out. The first time this happens, she simply tells her mother that her shirt is on inside out, just as she would for any of her friends. She has done it a time or two herself. The mother looks down, chuckles with a hint of embarrassment, fixes the shirt in the hallway mirror, and they move on like it was no big deal. But when it happens a second time shortly after, different shirt, same wardrobe rebellion, the daughter points it out again but this time with a slightly more careful tone. The mother frowns with a quick laugh and says, "Well, the other side had a spot on it." This habit becomes one of the many small cues that the daughter is starting to pay quiet attention to. But because the shirt ordeal isn't a crisis, only a moment, she knows that there is no need to disrupt their harmony over it, so she stops mentioning it altogether.

Some battles simply aren't worth fighting. So, the wisdom lies in discerning which hills are worth dying on. While seemingly insignificant matters may tempt intervention, true wisdom dictates prioritizing concerns that impact well-being and relationships instead of nitpicking along the way. This goes for both cognitive and physical changes.

For cognitive changes, think more along the lines of "I can't find my glasses," when they used to be able to find a needle in a haystack, or, "This doesn't taste like it used to," when that delicious signature homemade dish prepared the same way for years now hits the taste buds a little different. It could be forgetting evident details of recent events, and when the refrigerator becomes "that thing in the kitchen," maybe your parent begins to second guess their once-steadfast decision-making abilities or struggles to follow a rapid conversation. Consider the stove or oven that was left on; it may not be all the time, just enough to make you jump every time the smell of slightly burnt toast is in the air. All of these signs could remain harmless for many years and not require your immediate attention. However, the importance is in the acknowledgement that they are signs and believing that the wisdom is in understanding when to intervene, such as if their well-being or relationships are diminishing.

In terms of physical changes, maybe your parent isn't able to untighten a lid or firmly hold a filled coffee mug. They may stumble a bit more easily, or complain of aches and pains that never seemed to be bothersome before. Perhaps they fail to (or forget to) make a doctor's appointment because "it's not that bad." They may sit longer than usual in one place because the effort of moving outweighs the reason for getting up, and when they do need to move, they require help to get to a standing position. They may struggle with tasks that were once second nature, like tying shoes or driving at night. You notice their usual pride in their appearance now presents as wrinkled clothes, and the usual tidiness of the home is now marred by mounds of mail and beyond-parched houseplants. These are all indicators that something may be amiss, something that requires attention but not intervention—yet. For example, don't point out their wrinkled shirt, but if they complain of their arthritis flaring up, you can tactfully help them seek options that focus on their physical comfort (well-being).

Let's say that years have passed, and these subtle signs have finally reached the point that you are getting concerned about their well-being and relationships. For example, noticing that your parents have skipped church for the last few weeks, which is their main social circle, or they've tripped going up the steps a handful of times just this month. You may be thinking, "Okay, I've noticed significant shifts, and I'm beginning to worry. Now what?" With the goal of working toward a resolution and maintaining transparency, it's time to talk with your parents about what you're seeing.

 Avoid only covertly side-eying the hefty moonwalking elephant in the room, because the shift may not be as obvious to your parent.

Instead, directly bring up the elephant in the room, as this transparency can aid in minimizing awkwardness and can be a building block toward enhancing trust. But keep in mind, you aren't paparazzi or an investigator; just bring it to their attention in a curious, caring, and gentle way.

Remember that observation list? Well, if you've written down a couple things that concern you, whether they started out subtly but have worsened or immediately caught your attention, but you still don't know if it's time to take action, I recommend now asking yourself:

Are they still able to manage their personal hygiene safely (think shower safety)?

Possible solutions:

- Install safety equipment like grab bars, non-slip mats, and a shower bench.
- Consider a handheld shower head to improve ease and reduce fall risk.
- If mobility is a concern, look into hiring in-home assistance for bathing support a few times a week.
- Schedule a home safety assessment through their primary care provider or local agency on aging.

Can they prepare their own meals (think energy to shop or make meals)?

Possible solutions:

- Set up a grocery delivery or meal kit service tailored to seniors.
- Cook and freeze meals together for easy reheating later.
- Connect with programs like Meals on Wheels America for hot meal delivery options for seniors.
- If kitchen safety is a concern, reduce stove use and provide a microwave-safe meal plan.

Are they managing their medications correctly (think double dosing or missing a dose)?

Possible solutions:

- Use a clearly labeled pill organizer (weekly or monthly).

- Set up digital medication reminders via phone apps, smart speakers, or alarms.
- Request blister packs or bubble packaging from the pharmacy.
- Consider a medication management service or in-home assistance for check-ins if errors persist.

Is the home safe and accessible (think rails and steps)?

Possible solutions:

- Schedule a home safety assessment through their primary care provider or local agency on aging.
- Install stair rails, wheelchair ramps, brighter lighting, and motion sensor lights.
- Clear clutter and secure loose rugs or cords that could be tripping hazards.
- Investigate home modification grants or programs from local health departments or nonprofits.

Can they handle their finances without assistance (think deciphering phishing emails and phone scammers)?

Possible solutions:

- Set up online banking with alerts so you can monitor unusual activity.
- Use automatic bill pay for recurring expenses.
- Hold regular "money check-ins" together to review statements and spots inconsistencies.
- Introduce scam education resources and consider a

trusted financial power of attorney if judgment appears compromised.

These are just a few of the many questions you can consider, with possible solutions, when gauging whether it's time to address issues beyond just acknowledging the shift exists. Be prepared for a variety of outcomes within yourself—the answers might be uncomfortable and could even force you to confront the reality of situations that you've been ignoring either intentionally or unintentionally. So, accepting that your observation list and this initial assessment aren't just a checklist; they're a starting point for an exploratory conversation about options and will help you transition into this new phase more smoothly. Embrace it as a process of collaboration between you, your parents, and possibly other family members. And, because splitting responsibilities is often easier than attempting to shoulder the burden alone, involving siblings early on is crucial, even if it feels awkward or contentious.

 Sharing this responsibility not only lightens the load but also helps prevent resentment and burnout.

If you have a sibling(s) caring for your parents but live farther away from your parents than they do, you can still be more involved than providing the statement, "I wish I was there so I could do more." It can be an emotional challenge to be concerned and hopeless far away. As soon as you begin to think outside the box and see all the things you can do from your distance, this knowledge may fill you with a different kind of relief. Asking a sibling or family member, who is beginning to help your parents out more or has even become their full-time primary caregiver, for an assignment or a long-term responsibility is a good place to start. And when they give you that assignment, accept it graciously. Think auto-shipment of needed items, such as adult incontinence underwear, their favorite body wash, or a weekly professional housekeeping service. Or you might take on the role of care scheduler. You could manage upcoming appointments with a digital calendar that you and your sibling access. This saves your caregiving sibling valuable time and ensures that important dates don't get missed. Gestures like these can assist the parent and the caregiving sibling because it's one less thing that needs to be done.

Realistic, open, and honest conversations with siblings about how the daily responsibilities will be split, like who will drop off dinner, pop in to do dishes, or take the trash bins to the curb, will keep everyone on the same page and updated on the parents' well-being. So, don't be afraid to be the one to start these conversations—and definitely don't be afraid to ask for help! For example, "Hey, I was at Mom's house last night for dinner, and I noticed that her fridge was pretty empty. I'll be at work all day today, but could you stop by the store and grab some essentials? I can do a more extensive grocery shopping this weekend." That way, when support traverses into the more serious phases (which will be touched on in a later section) when your parents are needing more help, such as navigating financial priorities, daily check-ins, or hourly care, there is more familiarity because they were involved during the subtle shifting stages.

If you are the main caregiver in your family and you decide to begin the conversation with others in the family (siblings, for example), it is best to prepare yourself for a variety of reactions, including the tough ones like "I had no idea" or, "Why didn't you tell me?" There's the "I'm too busy" excuse, the "I can't afford it" stance, or the classic "no-response" deflection. Navigating these family dynamics requires patience, transparency, and a healthy dose of diplomacy. Add a well-placed guilt trip or two, depending on how much your sibling understands the seriousness of the situation. If you are the one most involved with offering support to your parent, you may not receive this next suggestion well, and you'll probably follow it up with a "Great, one more thing to add on my endless list." Here's the thing: you, being the primary support person, hold the responsibility of communicating all the details, even though adding this one more thing to your list seems like a herculean effort.

The alternative to failing to communicate with your siblings or connected family could result in shock, judgment, demands for explanation, or projecting blame your way because they didn't experience the progression of need. Although these reactions are unfair and may only stem from being told information that feels out of the blue, the exchange may get emotionally charged and hurtful. This breeds counterproductivity, thus detracting from a solution-focused outcome for your parent. Not to mention the added emotional pressure you now feel from thinking you've let others down while you're doing your best.

Although many may assume that the necessity of communicating with family members is obvious, much of what is offered in this book comes from the results of mine and others' attempts to get to the root cause of the oddities that occur, failed attempts at addressing them, and the lessons learned. It was all of us *learning the hard way* that trying to finesse our way toward getting answers with gentle curiosity doesn't always come naturally. But it shouldn't take continuous trial and error to connect with your parents in the way they need during this phase of their life, so by sharing my failed attempts and how I learned to pivot, my hope is that you can skip multiple attempts, and instead, be able to confidently embrace this new responsibility, all while leaving your parents with the independence and dignity they deserve.

When I first attempted to address my worries with my parents, my responses were often fueled by fear, frustration, and heightened concern. My emotions were elevated, much like the fear of seeing a young unsupervised child approach an expressway. When your parent denies, deflects, or rewrites history mid-sentence, it's easy to go from calm to

 "Okay, what level of nonsense is this today?"

But this isn't a cross-examination; it's a gentle negotiation with someone who thinks they definitely didn't leave the stove on. So, as much as possible, skip the hand flailing and courtroom tone, and instead of saying, "Don't you remember...?" or, "You forgot," try something like, "Sometimes I hit those 'meh' days too. You know what I found works for me to help me remember to turn the stove off? I put a dish towel over my shoulder while I cook. Even if I walk away from the stove, I'll eventually notice the towel over my shoulder, and it reminds me to check the stove."

Keep in mind, tone and body language matter tremendously. Take inventory of yourself to truly hear how you sound and to evaluate your posturing to ensure that there is congruency. For instance, you may sound calm, but if your lips are twisted and your forehead is scrunched up, you could still be sending a signal of annoyance. Do you present with a hand on your hip or with an arms-crossed, impatient stance? Approach sensitive topics with kindness, empathy, and with a nonintrusive posture, such as:

- **Soft eye contact** rather than an intense and unwavering gaze.
- **Uncrossed arms and legs** to signal openness and emotional availability.
- **Slight lean forward** while seated to show engagement and interest.
- **Relaxed hands and facial expression** with your hands in your lap or gently at your side while avoiding a furrowed brow.
- **Sit at the same eye level** as your parent, ideally side by side or at a slight angle. Standing over someone or sitting too far above them can unintentionally communicate dominance or a power imbalance.

Be sure to complete a visual scan of your body to ensure that you are facing your parent with a relaxed and physically interested openness. This is especially important with those that may already feel frustrated, embarrassed, and vulnerable. These are compassionate ways to express disquietude, curiosity, or redirection without being curt or condescending. After all, remember when they danced to The Doobie

Brothers wearing matching leather jackets that squeaked when they hugged? Today, they may be rocking compression socks and dread scammer phone calls, but that spirited smooth groove is still in there.

The "I'm Fine" Era: Where Everything Clearly Is Not Fine

This isn't chicken soup; it's gumbo, baby! Supporting parents through the aging process is thick, complex, and built on a slow simmered roux of emotions, patience, and learned experiences. The process isn't easy every time—it's one that uses each attempt to develop real, meaningful traction to get to that point where it is deeply nourishing. This journey is fraught with twists and turns that may leave you feeling Twilight Zone disoriented and dumbfounded, but there are things you can do to help yourself get through the rough times.

In my youth, my mother regularly watched the 1980s sitcom *M*A*S*H*, which was set during the Korean War and followed a fictional army unit of medical staff. I reveled in the joy of watching it with her because it sometimes gave me the chance to stay up late. But I also remember that I was unable to grasp laughter over a blood-soaked body on an operating table when the laugh track sounded. Now, in my adult, experienced disposition, I completely understand the sitcom and can see why my mom found it worth it to let me stay up with her to watch it. The whole show was about finding humor and togetherness during the stress of war while the characters dealt with matters in their personal lives. It was the camaraderie and humor that got them through the rough times. Taking those lessons from the TV and applying them to the hard moments of caring for an aging parent, you'll see that it's levity that just may be what gets us to a brighter day, even when the changes become more significant and begin affecting their personality.

These personality shifts may catch you off guard, especially if your focus has only been on them not dropping another glass plate or tripping on the threshold lip when going in and out of the front door. It can be jarring and unsettling when the stoic, self-sufficient parent who never asked for help becomes emotionally volatile, prone to fits of angst or sudden aloofness.

> *You see it, you feel it, you inquire about it, and the response you get is, "I'm fine."*

That's when the *really* unexpected challenges emerge, when you cannot help as you so desperately want to. Because, well, they're "fine."

Take this story for example: a woman raised three children practically single-handedly, was a business owner, and maintained a mortgage. As she aged, her sense of normalcy and abilities declined. While she wouldn't openly admit it, now in her 80s, she is more dependent on the assistance of others to simply help her navigate the nuances of life; for instance, the multitude of times her son has had to help her reset her bank password because she swears "they keep changing it." However, when there is an attempt to assist her, it becomes a battle of wills because her mission is to present as capable in the presence of her son. These situations can feel like a daily psychological standoff, full of trying patience, bafflement, and silent sighs as a context bubble above your head counts down from 10.

If they brush off your help, don't push back too hard—even if they used to openly accept it. Keep that emotional response leveled; this isn't about simple stubbornness. It's often a complex cocktail of pride, fear of losing independence, and a deeply ingrained sense of self-reliance. Instead, focus on offering support in small, nonintrusive ways, like helping with groceries, laundry, or other errands. To make them feel less like a burden, you could say, "I'm headed to the store, can I pick you up something while I'm there?" Ask if you can take them to doctor's appointments so you two can get coffee together afterward, or be present during an important phone call without drawing attention to it. By being there, they'll know they can ask you a question if they need to, but they won't feel like your help is out of their control. Besides, customer service representatives can talk too fast, making it hard for the elderly to not only understand them but to keep up. It is assumed that they are all tech savvy as well, being able to complete two-way authentication and upload needed documents. But clearly, I digress. The point is, these small acts of assistance can often reveal more than if you had a direct confrontation with this parent that would inevitably crash and burn.

Try not to win the battle. Instead, try to understand the war and be strategic. Your parents aren't rejecting your efforts; they're rejecting the loss of control, concerned that they are a burden, or simply grappling with the unavoidable realization of their own mortality. It's a natural—albeit painful—stage of aging. We, as their children, have a responsibility to navigate this delicate balance between providing necessary support and not standing in the way of them keeping their crown. The trick lies in finding creative compromises, offering help indirectly, and framing assistance as collaboration rather than intervention. You can say, "Hey, Mom, I made way too much lasagna. Can I stop by and give you some of this so it doesn't go to waste?" You can also try, "Hey, Dad, I have a free Saturday, and I'm looking for something to get me out of the house. Can I come over and help with that yard work? I don't have a hose at my apartment either, so could I use yours to wash my car? I can do yours too, while I'm at it." You understand that they have tasks that need to be completed, and you are asserting support while also letting them know they can still help you in some way as well.

Good Intentions And A Tough Crowd

Do you remember when options weren't optional? Growing up, I was pretty much a city recreation poster child. If there was a sport or activity, my siblings and I were there. Soccer, flag football, basketball, hockey, volleyball, baseball, swimming; if there was a sign-up sheet, I was on it. Not because I always begged to join, but because my parents decided I would. That was just the way it worked, back then. There was no inspirational "choose your own path" discussion. You got signed up, you showed up, snagged one of the provided t-shirts, and you didn't dare quit unless you had a loose limb. Did I love it all? Mostly yes. I had great coaches, made friends, and learned life lessons. But I will share this, though: I hated indoor soccer. But I was raised on the mantra of, "Once you start something, you finish it."

Options—we didn't get those. We were raised on obligation, playing to win, and Kool-Aid.

Fast forward to present day, where we're now the ones making the decisions with our parents. When it comes to supporting them, the instinct to take over can be strong. We may think, "I'll just figure it out…I'll handle it…I know what's best." But here's the thing: they're not kids. They aren't you in shin guards being dragged into something they don't love because they need to experience a variety of activities and learned skills. They've earned their parental crown and their choices, so before you go into protective overdrive, take a step back and pace the landscape. Ask yourself, "Have I included them in this decision?" They've earned the dignity of input, the freedom to complain, the respect of collaboration, and yes, even the right to hate indoor soccer. And let me tell you, if anyone demanded every ounce of that freedom to complain and the dignity of input—even at her own detriment—it is my mother-in-law. Honoring someone's autonomy gets a real workout when the person you're trying to support thinks your "help" is just a thinly veiled eviction notice.

My 80-year-old mother-in-law is a woman of strong convictions and a volume setting that rarely dips below "firmly assertive." So, after her partner passed away, and it became clear she could no longer manage her five-bedroom home alone, my husband presented the idea of her moving into a smaller apartment, closer to us. She responded to him with the same energy one might reserve for an IRS audit.

My husband, who deserved a lifetime supply of earplugs and stress-relief tea, made efforts to explain her reality, initially to no avail. The intentions behind his efforts had sound logic, keeping in mind that it was a necessary discussion since she had no local support (all family members lived out of state), and she was unable to financially keep up with her rent and utilities alone. But when his mother's emotions began to flail, he realized that his urging logic needed to lay low. Especially when he noticed a pattern beginning to surface—during various efforts to speak with her, she started reflecting over the years spent raising children and watching grandchildren in the home. She brought up moments when she'd welcomed people over for a good meal, late-night card games, and comfort in a carefree environment.

 She was holding on to the nostalgia of having a house full of children and grandchildren, even though it was well beyond a foregone reality.

So, it wasn't just her house she was being asked to give up. It was all the memories and potential that went with it.

This led my mother-in-law to sternly minimize the seriousness of her situation. When my husband would reason again, she reargued. He continued to point out the math, and somewhere between her declaratory chant of "Hell no, I won't go!" and his mathematical spreadsheet of doom, after nearly three months of my husband's persistent patience, *she* made the decision to leave the home. She had always understood the direness of her situation but needed time to *emotionally* move on. I don't know anyone that enjoys moving, so add in the component of aging, upending decades of normalcy, and now having to depend on others, it can be tough.

This is not a situation where you "play to win" by forcing your help on them and making choices for them that only you think are best. Instead, be patient—even if you see the emergency in bright, blinking neon lights. Try not to panic over their impending welfare decline; instead, comfort them as they try to relinquish some of the control that can be lost with aging. Frankly, there could be a lot to sort out (and I'm not just referring to throwing out "just in case" kitchenware and a fragmented encyclopedia collection). Much like my mother-in-law, your parent may need time to process the reality of the change needed. They could be holding on to a legacy of not just their belongings but what they see as their whole identity.

When The Shift Hits The Fan

At first, it was small things—forgotten appointments and odd fashion choices—but now, we're beyond the land of "subtle shifts." We've crossed into the territory of canceled utilities, disappearing medications, and a level of confusion that feels less charming and more concerning. You keep telling yourself you can balance it all because there's a visceral, albeit irrational, hope that it was just an illusion. That is, until the go-to calendar, refrigerator sticky notes, and gentle reminders are no longer working, and you have no choice but to grip reality, understanding that your parent requires more than the usual rigmarole of guidance and a supportive phone call.

This lesson especially hits home for me. You don't know what you don't know, and at the time, there were signs that my mother needed my assistance, but I hadn't caught them in time. It all started when my mother was prescribed medication for hypertension and swore she was perfectly capable of managing her medication. One day, after about six months of her taking her medication, I called her as usual only to hear her slurred speech and disorientation. I frantically hung up to call 911 and raced to her house. Shortly after paramedics arrived, we learned she'd suffered a stroke.

Thinking back to before the stroke, I was consumed with memory recall flashbacks where she was easily winded; the swelling of her body that was more than just weight gain; too many instances of eating out or eating not so good. I missed multiple opportunities to speak to her about her health. The stroke limited her use of the left side of her body, rendering her incapable of full independence. Because of this, she had to move into my home, and it wasn't easy for her to adjust to her limitations. Her regret was obvious, and all we could do at the moment was support this next chapter of her life. My regret? Not paying attention to the signs or asking the right questions. This experience shifted the dynamic of the usual support into full throttle.

This is when the *shift hits the fan* and turns into full acceleration. You realize that you are not just a supportive voice on the other end of the line; you are the de facto project manager of unchartered territory.

And yes, you still have your own life, your job, and your fully grown adult meltdown brewing quietly behind your eyes.

But intervention is now required, real plans, real conversations, and real help. The good news? This level of chaos is survivable. The better news? You don't have to navigate it alone.

Depending on your family dynamics, it might be helpful to have a structured plan, even a written proposal, to present to your siblings (and/or other family) before you begin the discussion. You might bring up topics like building or installing a mobility ramp for the home or taking your parent to the movies or on a walk weekly. Then, after presenting the list of options, ask who can take on each activity, and perhaps alternate who does what occasionally so no one gets burnt out in a specific area. As for me and my siblings, we stay pretty connected. If there is a change in the norm with our parents, before any in-person conversations take place, we send text messages to each other to soft launch the topic. To prevent messages from containing emotional overload, we simply let each other know what happened and begin a discussion about when we can get together and explore solutions. In the past, this message has looked something like this: "Hey, guys, just letting you know, Mom had a stumble getting out of the shower. She's okay, but I'm thinking we need to talk about outfitting the bathroom with more safety bars to prevent a fall." Either way, find what works for you and your family. Communication demonstrates your seriousness and commitment to finding a solution that benefits everyone involved.

Once you've assessed your parents' needs, and if the needs require more than what you and your family can offer, start exploring available resources. As the research phase of your care begins, remember that you don't have to handle this step alone; as with all the other items, start dishing out assignments. Always be prepared for the question, "Do you need anything?" The answer: "Yes, would you mind calling the local senior center to find out what is offered?"

Deciding on the best resource can be like wandering a maze blindfolded; don't let it paralyze you. To start, I recommend finding out what Medicare, Medicaid, Social Security, Veterans Affairs and the like will pay for and advocate for this care. What I've found is that there may be service-level support offered by medical insurance entities in your area that you weren't aware of, such as transportation assistance. Therefore, it may take genuine resource exploration to see every service available to your parents, even with a lack of marketing. As another example, I found out from a discussion with someone in line at the grocery store that Medicare covers activities that encourage healthy aging. I returned home on the hunt like a seasoned detective. I reviewed the multi-paged encyclopedia-sized annual coverage of benefits and found out that Medicare offers programs like fall prevention safety and activities that promote cognitive stimulation.

I try to remember that the reality is that most insurance companies lean toward "no" first and make you work for their approval of services, including requiring a referral from a primary care physician. So, all you can do is advocate, push assertively, and be prepared to do so from the start. Keep in mind that outside of medical insurance, paying for these services is always an option, if your circumstances are amenable to it.

One quick note about paying for services: I don't believe that it's a good idea to sign any financial document that leaves you as the person responsible for your parent's debt unless absolutely necessary. If your parent is able to understand the process and responsibilities involved, even if it takes you explaining it in plain speak, have your parent sign. You can still provide guidance that helps them manage their financial priorities without breaking *your* bank. If needed, you can still assist by paying the bills *for* them, along with your siblings, while avoiding financial responsibility. Being that you are most likely managing the other hats you may wear, like marriage, bills, children, a career, pinching pennies is most likely one of your survival talents. Being a support and advocate doesn't have to mean footing the bill.

While not a complete and comprehensive list, there is a short list of resources below to consider for aging parents, with a longer list in the back of the book for an even deeper dive:

In-home care: This could be daily hours of assistance with food preparation, transportation, bathing, toileting, and dressing to having a full-time aid. These resources typically provide lower income elderly adults assistance in the home because in the absence of this support, they would most likely be in out-of-home care.

Consider the pros and cons:

- **Pros**: Your parents remain in the comfort of their home; they will have personalized one-to-one care; there would be greater family involvement and peace of mind; and there will be reduced exposure to illness.
- **Cons**: The cost; if income exceeds government-assisted allowances; having a stranger in the home; and the availability of qualified caregivers.

You might find it helpful to speak with some home health agencies and compare services, pricing, and the availability of services. You should also carefully screen any potential caregiver. This option could lighten the load for family members trying to manage care on their own. That way, when you do visit with your parent, there is an opportunity to avoid the regimen of a "check-in" visit and just have a meaningful, caring exchange with them.

Monitoring services: These can be anything from a nanny camera to a service provider monitoring service. A nanny camera is a small surveillance camera that is Wi-Fi-enabled and can be used to monitor the well-being and safety of your parent. Many models offer features like two-way audio, motion alerts, night vision, and cloud recording. Provider monitoring services usually include a direct line to emergency assistance or to a family member, while a nanny camera usually provides the basic visual feed, but is more cost-effective.

Senior/retirement living communities: This option is best suited for independent individuals who seek a more social and active lifestyle. It allows for continued independence while offering the benefit of a higher level of socialization, which counters the isolation of living alone. These communities typically do not offer assistance with daily living or medical care.

Assisted living/nursing home facilities: Nursing homes provide comprehensive medical care for individuals who require significant assistance with daily living activities, such as bathing, toileting, dressing, and medication management. This resource is a good choice even if your parent only needs this level of care temporarily. For example, roughly 12 years after my mother's stroke, she had a horrible fall from an unobstructed standing position and broke her pelvis and fractured her clavicle bone. She was unable to do anything without assistance. From the emergency department, she was transferred (with Medicare approval) to a rehabilitative nursing facility. There was a full nursing staff, a doctor that completed weekly rounds, physical therapists, occupational therapists, and general staff to handle meals and maintenance. She eventually was stable enough to return home. However, everyone's circumstances are different, and this situation could result in long-term care for your parent.

Prioritize facilities with high ratings and a strong reputation. Typically, these homes are regulated by government entities, which means they have standardized requirements that must be met. However, they all can have varying ranges of attentiveness and care. Visit in person and ask your parent what their take on the environment is. Smell, listen, and observe the environment, the staff's interactions with residents, and the cleanliness of the facilities.

This option can be pretty pricy and financially unattainable without insurance, but don't let this discourage you. First, if your parent has insurance in place, ensure that the facility is aware of the coverage. But if not, there may be other suitable options that can meet your parent's needs by using a combination of other resources, such as in-home healthcare with a monitoring service.

In YOUR home care: Having your parent under your roof means less 3 a.m. worry spirals and more peace of mind. You see what they're eating (or not eating), you can celebrate their small steps of progress or catch issues before they capsize, and you can be the monkey wrench thrown between phone impersonation scammers and your parent. There is a significant amount of information online that points to ways the elderly fall victim to scammers and suffer financial losses, such as mail order marketing, tech support scams, and even romance scams. Scammers prey on the elderly with confusing or misleading tactics because of their cognitive decline, because they have a higher chance of living in isolation, and because they tend to endure the pressure from scammers because they may be too polite or trusting. Having your parent in your home can seriously reduce outside risks from predatory phone scammers to late-night ordering binges that result in things like a collection of kitchen knives marketed to chop down a redwood tree. It's also easier to coordinate appointments, medications, and their impulsive inclinations, like performing yard work with the streetlights on.

You're no longer coordinating care from a distance, allowing you to gain real-time insight into their needs and abilities. You know when they're slipping (literally), when they're thriving, and when they should relax. However, just as all of these options, there's another side of *in your home care* to prepare for: that same proximity that lets you be a part of your parent's best days also means you're now on the receiving end of every complaint, refusal, minimization, opinion, and unsolicited parenting critique. You've also added a permanent backseat driver to your marriage. Your home is now a multi-generational sitcom, with you playing the role of referee, project manager, and reluctant tech support.

Senior community centers: Whether they live on their own or have moved in with you, these centers provide a daytime place for your parent to socialize and engage in activities with their peer group. Some of these centers either offer transportation or can assist with transportation resources. They might provide food options and additional assistance for adults with limited mobility, as well.

Seeking this option can provide consistent stimulation and socialization for your parents while giving the caregiver some respite during the week, but even if you view this as the best route, still lead with compromise and forgo coercion. When broaching this idea for the first time, especially with parents that are resistant to trying a new environment, try not to present it as a forced decision or an ultimatum. It may even be helpful to drop into the center with them to take a look around so you don't spend as much time trying to convince them of the positives.

I recommend booking the tour while running other errands, such as eating out or grabbing groceries (or another activity that your parent enjoys), so it doesn't feel like the sole purpose of your day together, which will lessen the pressure they feel. While exploring, engage with your parent by commenting on what you see and experience along the way. Who knows, they may run into an old friend and make an instant reconnection. Ask for a schedule of activities and find out what might pique your parent's interest. It may be a soft nudge and a compromise of a couple of days a week at first, so be patient and allow them to go at their own pace in the decision-making process.

If your parent makes a remark like, "I don't need anything, and there's nothing I want to do there. I'm fine," after your attempt to invite them to check out that senior community center, you could try a more explorative reply, like: "No part of you is even a *little* curious about what's available or what could make life lively? Could we at least check it out and see if you change your mind? And if not, hey, at least we saw it for ourselves." Let their response stand, and nudge the topic again at a later time if it's appropriate. No matter what the problem is, remember: you're there to support not to nag. Share your observations and concerns in small doses. Don't take their disinterest personally.

And if your parent absolutely refuses the senior center, still refrain from pushing! Instead, gently remind them it's just an option, then let the idea settle like a seed that might bloom later. You're planting a possibility, not issuing a command, and sometimes, that's enough to spark curiosity later on in their own time. Like my mother-in-law, when my husband wanted her to move closer and she first needed time to emotionally adjust to the change. Until they embrace readiness, cherish the little wins, like if they've maintained their commitment to the houseplants or still pay attention to the cat—it still counts as some level of engagement.

Even with this short list, it's easy to get lost within the mass translation of resource qualifications or ignite a course of strong advocacy for your parent, so applying options to your specific family situation, building a strategy, and maintaining a realistic outlook on a process as unpredictable as aging itself could be deflating. Which is why it's important to not hesitate in seeking help from social workers, elder law attorneys, or an ombudsman who specializes in navigating the complexities of elder care. These professionals can provide valuable assistance with understanding your options and advocating for your parents' needs. So, grab that coffee (what I endearingly refer to as my cup of cuddly), take a deep breath, and remember, you're doing amazing, even if your eye twitched once or twice.

"Sarcasm is not a love language."

Two
. . .

Respecting Who They Were While Loving Who They're Becoming

WHEN I WAS GROWING UP IN MY PARENT'S HOUSEHOLD, THERE were some pretty clear "nevers":

Never leave a light on in a room you aren't in.

Never hold the refrigerator door open for too long.

Never forget to lock the front door.

Now, I've taken on the role my parent used to have with me in my youth. It's a crazy mind trip, and sometimes I sit back and just chuckle. Especially when I see one of those Progressive Insurance commercials that depict examples of how people transition into acting like their parents. I find myself expending cautionary care reminders—"Please watch your salt and sugar intake" and, "You've been holding the fridge open for 10 minutes; are you having a hard time choosing?" Oh, and this one: "Be careful before you fall." Have you found yourself in this role?

In Chapter 1, I mentioned the importance of not telling your parents what to do, whether that's forcing them to do something or keeping them from doing something. But that being said, that mindfulness can be hard to maintain 24/7. For example, finding my father, who already has a wobbly gait, on a ladder, or pulling into his driveway to be immediately greeted by a chaotic whirl of yard work well after sunset, or my mother failing to take her medication—again. When did we convert into henpecking and helicopter parenting our parents? For a majority of us, it stems from concern, exasperation, a desire to support, and fear that something *else* will happen. Frankly, it feels like I've been running from the infamous "else" throughout this process. When those emotions erupt unfiltered, my communication skills fade in the wind, and I'm as supportive as strapless bra. I say things I *definitely* don't mean, and I harbor a lot of regret.

When we're exhausted, it's easy to lose our patience with others in our life, whether it's our partner, co-worker, or a stranger walking a little too slowly in the grocery aisle. It's no different when caring for our parents while depleted. It manifests in frayed nerves and terse interactions, making it easy to snap, to become impatient, and to let the pressure of daily demands erode the respectful communication that's so important to maintaining a healthy parent–child bond. Even during the most challenging moments, keeping your heart open and fostering positive memorable connections is paramount. This means actively working on our communication, becoming more mindful of our words and tone, and being intentional with our effort to understand what our parents are trying to communicate.

I'll share a personal example of how I learned this lesson. Roughly 12 years after my mother's stroke, she still required daily physical therapy exercises. Much of the exercises were designed for her to complete independently while she was alone during the day. The exercises required resistance activities, weights, and moderate walking around the house. As time went on, I lengthened the time between how often I inquired about her exercises, which led her to provide spontaneous updates without me asking. At one point, she admitted that she stopped doing her exercises. I became dismayed because I feared her mobility would further decline, and when I asked why, her answer was, "I keep forgetting." With an audibly humorous laugh laced in sarcasm, I said, "Come on, Mom, you act like your calendar is full. Seriously, how could you forget?" Another of her reasons for no longer exercising was, "It's not easy." My long, drawn-out, exasperated comeback was, "You're right. It's *physssss-ical* therapy."

Another one of my lackluster moments was one when my mother expressed her wish of being able to obtain her driver's license again [privileges revoked due to her stroke] and jump in her car "to just go when I want to." My retort, with affect as flat as day old soda: "Mom, you seem pretty okay with where you are now, because you aren't working to improve." It was this interaction that arrested me where I stood when I caught her heavy sigh and disheartened agitation. I literally forgot all manner in who I was talking to and attempted to backpedal with a fumbled apology, my words tripping over themselves as I scrambled to soften what had already landed too hard.

My responses were not supportive, they were not empathetic, and they were very much demotivating.

> *In short, sarcasm is not a love language, and I truly missed opportunities to deliver heartfelt moments of support.*

But I've learned to remind myself that this is all new for me too and that the best way to show I regret my previous reactions is to learn, grow, and offer more patience during the interactions that come afterward.

In my professional and personal landscape, I've been trained in understanding the importance of effective communication, reading a room, motivating others toward change, respecting autonomy, deciphering authenticity, and encouraging healthy risks. In the examples provided, those skills were wholly absent, and I had to stop and ask myself why my patience was wearing so thin and why all my practiced communication seemed to vanish in the heat of our conversations—she is my mom, after all. Shouldn't I have *more* patience? The truth was laid bare and grievous: I was wrestling with the difference between the vibrant woman who raised me and the version of her now slowly shifting before my eyes. I still see flashes of who she was, strong, joyful, unstoppable but they're just that now—flashes.

> *I'm slowly grieving the loss of who she used to be.*

Maybe you feel it too, the quiet heartbreak of loving someone who's still here, but not entirely the same.

In order to break the cycle, she needed me to share my fears and worries in a more productive way. I began to use more effective ways to communicate, and my interactions with my mother were transformed. For example, I started to slow down and simply ask, "Mom, how have you been feeling about your daily routine, lately?" Or, "What would make getting ready for exercises feel a little easier or more enjoyable?" Listen for the challenges, especially the unspoken challenges (and exasperated sighs), and offer encouragement. You should have compassion with no judgment, so the line of communication remains open. Such as, "Your day-to-day feels overwhelming right now. Like, your energy doesn't stretch as far as it used to." Approach the conversation with empathy while focusing on curiosity. This will translate to them as you asking because you truly care about their answer—not as if you are checking off a box on your to-do list.

Taking all that into consideration, it's also important to remember not to over-focus on their struggles or issues. What I mean by this is, even though consistent check-ins are important, I also recommend having interactions with them that aren't about their limitations or how they're feeling. Sauce it up a bit. I learned to mix in my mother's desire to give me details of her TV programming throughout the day with her feelings about exercising or whatever her focus was at the moment. So, after I calmed down my insensitivity toward her and encouraged a more natural conversation pattern between us, I found out that she was actually scared to perform exercises alone for fear that she would fall or hurt herself when no one was home. She didn't feel comfortable telling me this initially because she wanted to avoid my disappointment. That was a gut punch! She had one thing right; I was disappointed. But in myself, not her. I needed to slow down and put myself in her shoes, remembering that this level of new and unknown couldn't be easy for her.

If you and your parent can't relate to such an extreme example of at-home physical therapy, the importance of patience can show in smaller examples too. A common one that comes to mind is when you find yourself answering your parent's repetitive questions within a small window of time—this is when your temperament will really need to set in. If you're asked three times within an hour what time a doctor's appointment is, consider *just* answering it again instead of telling them they've now asked you three times,

 because sometimes it's better to be kind than honest.

All that being said, when your parent responds with an unhelpful dialogue, either an outright refusal of help or simply brushes you off, I encourage you to make efforts to find out their reason. You'll find that it could be a matter of not being ready to face the reality of requiring assistance, which can come across as pridefulness, stubbornness, or fear, which is a rush of emotions we've all experienced at one point or another. Most aging parents find it hard to seek assistance because for so long, they provided it to us; so instead of getting defensive, focus on offering support in segmented, nonintrusive ways. The key is to approach the conversation by explaining your purpose and ensuring that your tone and words come from a place of genuine support. Meaningful communication means creating a safe space for open dialogue and choosing the right time and place to have important conversations.

However, if you notice your parent is still struggling, even after you've stepped in to offer your reassurance, it may be time to reassess and adjust the level or type of support you're offering. Choose a calm, comfortable setting free from distractions, and give yourselves the time and space to talk without pressure or interruption.

Thoughtful, uninterrupted conversations can reveal what's working, what's not, and how to move forward with care.

Even then, expect some form of resistance.

Here's a breakdown of some techniques and reminders that were helpful to me and may prove to be useful to you:

Clear the air: It's important to make amends. If you've failed to take others' feelings into account or have even hurt someone's feelings along the way, first acknowledge the harm. This reminds me of one of my favorite quotes by Maya Angelou:

"...people will forget what you said, people will forget what you did, but people will never forget how you made them feel."

Relating this to your parent, let them know you acknowledge that you haven't done a winning job at listening, and then sincerely apologize. Make a passionate commitment to them that you will make a pointed effort to listen to their wants and to their needs.

Intentional listening: Now that you've cleared the air and established an approach that fosters collaboration rather than control, let's lean into intentional listening. This technique focuses on helping our parents feel more involved and less like a passive recipient of our care.

Intentional listening is more than just hearing words; it's about making deliberate efforts to understand the *emotions* behind those words. It's about paying attention, not just to what's being said, but also to *how* it's being said; the tone of voice, the body language, the unspoken looks of worry or general concern. Oftentimes, the most important communication isn't explicitly stated, it's conveyed through roundabout cues, such as a weighted downward look, pinched forehead, sunken posture, or microaggressions.

Have you noticed your parent withdrawing more from you? Are they less engaged in conversations than they used to be? It may be that we become lost in the daily interrogation of the checklist check-in. Meaning we've lost sight of these check-ins being for their benefit, and instead, we prioritize control of the situation, leading to intensity. Be patient, and let them express their concerns and anxieties within the conversation. Avoid interrupting or dismissing their feelings. Validation is important, even if you don't necessarily agree with their perspective. A simple, "I understand how frustrating that must be" can go a long way.

Join—don't judge: Join in the conversation to purposely understand the gamut of emotions and thoughts they could be feeling. It can be easy to formulate an opinion, cast judgment, and move into solving a problem all in the blink of an eye. Maintaining eye contact, offering a gentle touch, and using a calm, reassuring tone of voice can convey empathy and support. Attempting to be unbiased is very important, and it will prevent you from casting judgment prematurely. Avoid crossing your arms, rolling your eyes, or sighing loudly, as these can come across as dismissive or uncaring, even if unintentionally. Our body language speaks volumes; be conscious of the messages it sends.

"Join—don't judge" leaves room for you to learn more, join with those involved, and lean into the dilemma or concern. You can't effectively solve a problem if the involved people aren't at the table sharing in the discussion. After you understand your parent's concerns, frame your ask and offer of assistance in the form of support. Instead of saying, "You're not able to manage your finances anymore," try, "Mom, I've been worried about your bills lately. Would you be open to us looking at things together, just to make sure everything is running smoothly?" Then, continue with intentional listening to keep the dialogue going.

 This is about preserving the soul of who they are, even if life is reshaping what they can do.

Preserve dignity: Emphasize that the goal is to help them maintain independent choices and enhance their quality of life, not take it away. Even if some of their independence has been compromised already, keep in mind, there is usually some level of independence still left. So, as we talked about in our discussion of the importance of kind communication earlier, choose your words carefully, avoiding condescending language or making them feel insignificant. For example, instead of saying, "You're too old to live alone," and getting frustrated when that explanation isn't enough for them to agree with you, focus on what they're struggling with, such as moving into your home, while exploring options that preserve as much of their autonomy as possible.

Also, if you know your parent has incontinence issues or something similar (and they know you know) and you're going out with them, make it an easier adventure. Keep a bag in your car that has a change of clothing and necessary items in case there is an accident. You can position this sensitive topic in a way that you want to ensure they enjoy themselves. You can let them know that if something happens, you've got their back, their front, and their pride. Tell them you'll just pretend it was a spilled latte and keep it moving.

Patience and persistence: As was touched on earlier, be mindful not to get irritated, be cognizant of your body language, and have kind interactions. It may take multiple conversations to reach a consensus on most topics that require change. Don't get discouraged or frustrated if they initially resist. Additionally, if you know you have a tendency to fail at tempering your emotions during difficult times, take inventory of your physical stance. Make sure you do away with posturing body language because it could be interpreted as dominance. And try to avoid those infamous four words: "I told you so." These responses are discouraging, and you may find that your parent begins to hide their hardships from you because your condescension is the last thing they want to hear.

Dig deeper to understand, for example, why your father may refuse to use a cane, even after experiencing multiple falls. When you know their true feelings behind a topic and learn that, in this case, they have a strong opinion about something you thought was trivial, you have a better chance at finding common ground. Otherwise, you're forcing a Band-Aid on a bullet wound instead of addressing the core problem. In the case of the cane, you could learn that it's uncomfortable, he didn't find it helpful (showing you he may not know how to use it properly), or the more obvious, he finds it embarrassing to use. No matter what the reasoning is, it gives you a fair chance to fix the issue, leading to their improved sense of self and well-being.

It's also vital to not go into any conversation bombarding them with a laundry list of concerns. Instead, focus on one specific area at a time, like medication management, fall prevention, or meal preparation. Maybe start with a reasonable suggestion: "Would you be open to trying a pill organizer, or maybe I could help you set up a reminder on your phone?"

Exploring the positives and negatives of your recommendation, like using a cane or visiting a senior community center, could be more beneficial than insisting they must. And just as we talked about earlier when asking if they want to go to a senior center, it's important to respect their decision and not press the matter.

Conflict is inevitable in any close relationship, particularly one as complex as the parent–child dynamic during aging. Disagreements can be valuable learning opportunities, as long as they are handled with respect. Learning to navigate these conflicts constructively is essential for maintaining or enhancing a strong bond. Remember, it's about maintaining the relationship. Find common ground, even if it means slightly adjusting your approach or accepting a different solution.

Mistakes are bound to be made, but it's about being willing to learn and improve. You'll experience frustration, guilt, resentment, and moments of sheer exhaustion, but there will also be moments of connection, humor, and even profound gratitude. It's an unpredictable journey, but the goal is not rightness; instead, it's a consistent effort to communicate with empathy, patience, and understanding, ensuring that our parents feel loved, respected, and valued, even during the most challenging aspects of the aging process. Remember, your voyage is one shared by so many, and while the road ahead may not be paved with perfection, remember your era of resourcefulness (by age, experience, or attitude). We are survivors, we are adaptable, we can handle the hard stuff, and we shake it off as we get back up.

Caring For The Complicated

Recently, I reunited with Zamira, a friend from elementary school, after being separated for years. As we shuffled through catching up on foregone time, she opened up about her childhood. There was a time when her home always echoed with laughter, music, the feeling of comfort, and the smell of a Pine-Sol-cleaned house on Saturdays. Her parents were hard-working, middle-class providers. They were the quiet heroes in the kind of neighborhood where block parties stretched into the evening, and the biggest worry was whether the kids would come in before the streetlights came on. Birthdays and holidays were full of balloons, cousins, and friends. Celebrations meant the smell of birthday cake, card tables packed with food, cards, dominoes, and folding chairs overflowing with loving memories in the making. Zamira knew her parents weren't perfect, but they showed up, and for a while, that was more than enough.

Then the '80s arrived—not just with neon, lace, and breakdancing, but with something darker. Crack cocaine swept through neighborhoods like a tidal wave, erasing joy, jobs, and families in its path. Her parents, once the rock-solid center of the household, became shadows of themselves, gripped by an addiction so strong it silenced the once-vibrant hum of their home. The lights were often off, the fridge often empty. The eyes of her and her siblings lost their optimistic gleam as their days turned into uncharted landscapes. Social workers replaced sleepovers, and law enforcement welfare checks took over weekend outings. Eventually, Child Welfare Services were forced to step in even further, removing them from their parents, splintering everything in the process; her father imprisoned, her mother lost to the wind. For years, they were just pieces of a broken family, scattered by the impact of addiction and trauma.

As adults, her siblings had no interest in a parental reunion, but 17 years after being taken out of their home, Zamira had a desire to reunite with them. Maybe it was curiosity or hope that led her to her decision. With assistance from other family members, she found both parents in fragile states, living separate lives. Her father had a multitude of health problems, lived alone, and had been in recovery for several years. Her mother was homeless and continued to struggle with sustaining long-term sobriety despite substance use interventions. Zamira wanted to know and understand her parents more. So, with mixed feelings, she eagerly visited with her parents and slowly found herself stepping in to provide support and guidance.

She made weekly efforts to connect with her mother, some successful and some not. During those connections, her mother was often detached, showing little interest in rebuilding a bond. These efforts continued for a year, until her mother passed away from a drug overdose. As a result, Zamira was grief stricken from the melancholic loss of what could have been. But as time went on, Zamira continued to make connections with her father. She had already suffered the loss of one parent too soon, and with focused intensity, she did *not* want to miss an opportunity to re-bond with her father. Though he remained in recovery during their time of reconnection, his history of drug use resulted in declining health, which was coupled with behaviors indicative of aging shifts like an unsteady gait, compromised clarity, and an impatient attitude. Ultimately, she became his full-time caregiver, a role she had never asked for and often didn't want, but one she felt obligated to take, since he didn't have anyone else in his life. Torn between resentment, abandonment, responsibility, and fear of another parental loss, Zamira showed up every day. Some days, she showed up with patience, some days with a clenched jaw, but always with the reoccurring ache of someone still grieving what could have been.

 There's an unspoken heaviness that comes with caring for a parent who wasn't always there for you.

Maybe they were physically present but emotionally unavailable. Maybe they prioritized their vices over your needs. Maybe they just weren't the parent you hoped for, needed, or deserved. Now, as they age and need support, you're either being asked or expected to step in, feeling obligated to show grace to someone who may have never extended the same. So, this section is for Zamira and others stunted by the "what could've been." It's for the child who has tried to love a parent that let them down because they were incapable of being the parent they desperately needed them to be. It's a tough ask, and if no one else has said this yet: you are not a bad person for grappling with it.

Years of shared history don't always equal years of emotional closeness. Old wounds, unresolved resentment, and a lifetime of unmet expectations don't magically disappear just because your parent now needs help getting in the bed or to the bathroom. The truth is, caregiving for a parent who let you down is anything but simple. It's ugly, emotional, and often unfair. It forces you to hold two truths at once: they may not have been who you needed then, and even so, you're choosing to be there for them now. That choice doesn't require forgetting the past, but it may invite a reframing of it to understand and cope, not to excuse or erase.

But this process can also be where the healing begins. When you're caring for a parent who didn't show up for you emotionally or physically in your own childhood, there's an invisible, ardently charged, emotional elephant in the room. Coping starts with boundaries and honesty. Name your feelings and say them out loud to a friend, a therapist, or even on the Notes app on your phone. Unspoken feelings have a way of festering beneath the surface, often manifesting as irritability, resentment, fatigue, or guilt. When you don't allow your emotions healthy circulation, you cut off air supply—you suffocate them. Over time, what happens when air is trapped? It becomes stale, stank, and just funky. Metaphorically, you begin to approach life with a stale, stank, and funky attitude if you keep shelving those emotions. And naming your feelings gives you power over them instead of the other way around. Hopefully, by identifying your emotions and giving them space, you create room for both compassion and boundaries, two things essential for finding peace in this complex caregiving role.

 Caregiving doesn't mean becoming emotionally exposed to old pain without protection.

Create space for breaks, for saying no, and for keeping your heart safe. Know that support can be both logistical and limited; it doesn't have to be a reenactment of the nurturing you never received. Sometimes, offering care can be as simple and sacred as keeping someone safe, fed, and clothed without sacrificing your own well-being.

If you're ready to clear the air or make meaning of a complicated past with your parent, below are a couple of exercises that could help with this difficult reconnection.

The shared history exchange:

Set aside an afternoon with your parent somewhere quiet and free of distractions. Bring an old photo, or a memory, or even just two pens and two notebooks. For the old photo or memory, find one that resonates with you, either because it comes with a positive feeling or even resurfaces old wounds.

Both can be used as conversations starters to reflect on how they may have impacted both of you. If you choose one that is important but too painful, consider sidelining it until you feel an emotionally safe, healing-focused rapport has been established.

In processing the old photo or memory, try these questions if you get stuck: "Tell me about your favorite memory from your 20s." Conversely, "Tell me about the most challenging moment of your youth," or, "What do you think of when you look at this old picture?" Give yourselves as much time as you need to think of the answers, and then take turns verbally sharing them. Let the conversation evolve from there. You may learn more than you expected. If the space feels safe, share memories that are good, bad, and thorny. You don't need a perfect, picturesque reconciliation; sometimes, just being heard or finally hearing their side is enough make some room for healing.

If a verbal exchange is slow to evolve or stagnant, you can use the pens and notebooks. You can use the notebooks to jot down any questions you may have for each other and exchange them, similar to becoming pen pals. Your parent can answer your questions in the notebook, and you can answer theirs. Give each other time to finish writing the answers, and when you're both ready and comfortable, take turns sharing what you wrote. You can either do this in an allotted time, sitting at a table together, or you can extend the exercise, both of you taking the notebooks home to give yourselves a private moment to consider the questions and write your responses. Whether it's immediately or when you agree to meet again, when you're both ready to verbally discuss the written exchange, give it a try. If not, swap them again and continue the written exchange until the time becomes right.

Moving forward doesn't mean pretending the past didn't happen—it means deciding what now looks like, whether that's creating one new tradition, having a hard conversation, or simply choosing to sit beside them with more peace than bitterness. You are not obligated to rewrite history, but you do have the power to add a better chapter now.

Isolated time for reflection:

Take a quiet, personal moment to journal your reflections on your relationship with your parent. Not just as the caregiver you are now, but as the child you once were. There may be moments that still sting, memories that feel unfinished, and emotions that rise without warning. Let them, and memorialize them by writing those emotions in your journal. These are your private thoughts and reflections and do not have to be shared, so write them down uncensored. This journal is meant to be cathartic, and by honoring your experience and considering what healing looks like for you, it can be a renewing benchmark to begin moving forward. Here are some things you can ask yourself and respond to through journaling:

- What is one memory from childhood that still feels unresolved for me? What emotions does it bring up?
- How have I changed since then, and what boundaries or strengths do I have now as a result?
- What do I need from this caregiving experience in order to feel emotionally safe and respected?

- Is there anything I wish I could say to my parent, even if just on paper?
- What kind of relationship do I want to have with my parent now in this chapter of life? What would help me get there?

Caring for a parent with a complicated past requires emotional agility along with the ability to hold grief in one hand and compassion in the other. It means finding the balance between what was and what is and recognizing that growth can coexist with pain. You don't have to pretend the journey was smooth to be proud of how far you've come. This chapter isn't about posturing that trauma doesn't sting; it's about embracing what you've learned, choosing peace where possible, and allowing the next chapter to reflect your strength, not your scars.

 "You don't have to rewrite the past to write a beautiful ending."

—Anonymous

Celebrating Memories And Creating New Ones

My parents divorced when I was in middle school. My siblings and I primarily lived with our mom and visited with our dad after he recovered from multiple days of 12-hour shift work. As for my mom, she worked two jobs and was sometimes so tired that when she slept, I was certain an earthquake couldn't wake her. So, while this was a rare occurrence, I did exploit the limited amount of supervision and energy a single-parent household tends to provide and did things I definitely shouldn't have. But as I discovered, I would always get caught in the end, and there are few moments in life more humbling than being 16, grounded, and forced to confess your sneaky sins to your dad on speakerphone while your mom holds you in place like a hostage.

One time, this happened after a night when I only had one goal: to attend the party of the moment, the kind with no parents, alcohol, and a backyard full of bad decisions. But my mom, a woman whose rules were ironclad, had already responded to my ask to go out and replied, "Are you crazy? Hell no!" in that tone that meant try it and die. I rationalized that because she slept like a tranquilized bear, and since the party was in the neighborhood, I could sneak out of my window, slip through the front yard side gate, head down the driveway, and return the same way without her knowing, just like the stealthy ninja Snake Eyes from G.I. Joe. What I didn't count on was her best friend, our next-door neighbor, eyeing me walk down my driveway as she pulled into *her* driveway coming home. I froze in place, my mouth open in shock, as my friends that waited for me across a darker part of the street remained oblivious to the impending untethered rage I knew was coming from my mother in 10, 9, 8, 7, 6…

I swear, my mom's best friend full-on sprinted inside her house to call her. Standing outside in the silence of the eerie night as I held my sudden fear-struck urge to pee, less than 10 seconds passed before I heard my house phone ring, and out of nowhere, I saw my enraged mom storming toward me. My friends scattered but not before my mother yelled, "Oh, I see all of you out there, and you better get home, because I'm calling parents tonight!" I got dragged inside to receive my world's worst punishment. My mom called my dad and made me tell him everything I had done while she hoovered over me with a homicidal glare. I was always labeled the responsible one; the one that could be depended upon. So, to admit to my rogue behavior—especially to my dad, who held me in high regard—left me feeling mortified. I never attempted to sneak out of the house again.

Now, my mom and I laugh about it, hard. Here's the surprising part: telling that story again as an adult somehow made us closer. It was a reminder that I was a kid, and she was the parent, just trying to keep me safe with the tools she had (and a very loyal and nosy neighbor). These moments, once shame-filled for me, have become tiny bridges between who we were and who we are now.

Revisiting that story led to me asking her about stories from her youth. I've been able to learn about her more and hear her memories about the escapades of other family members. My suggestion would be to open that door first and show your vulnerability. Lowering your guard could welcome them to do the same. These moments of mutual confession, mine with less drama now, and hers with surprising Cajun spice, have deepened our bond in unexpected ways. So, ask them what they got away with (or didn't), and you share what they never knew about you.

 The retelling and sharing of stories has a different conveyance the second time around.

If you're having a hard time getting started or knowing what kinds of questions to ask, try these ones, catering them to fit your situation if needed:

- "Okay, be honest. What's something you did as a teenager that would've made Grandma faint?"
- "When you were a kid, what did you definitely think you were going to be when you grew up?"
- "Was there ever a moment when you realized your parents were just human, trying to do the best they could?"
- "Tell me a funny or interesting story about Aunt Rose that she'd never share with me."

I encourage you to get bold with your questions. Be silly, and sincere. This isn't about conducting a formal oral history—it's about sitting in comfortable space with a literal or metaphorical photo album on your lap and a cup of something warm in your hand, and letting the stories find you. The beautiful part is, the more stories we share, the more human we all become to each other. I stopped seeing my parents solely as disciplinarians or providers and began to see the full arc of their lives. I saw the mischief, the big dreams, the pain, and the triumphs. The decades between us suddenly folded up like origami, and there we were, just people sharing beautiful elements of our lives. When your parent shares this part of their life with you, receive it like a gift. Reminiscing about the past is important to strengthen the present, and so is what you're building together now. Your presence with them matters, and you may not be able to dedicate as much time as you'd like, so make the moments memorable.

These exercises can happen anywhere, including during a walk through the neighborhood, a drive with no destination, or breakfast at a diner, all of which could have an uplifting impact on your parent. Aim for the imperfect, spontaneous bursts of connection that become part of the story you're still writing together. Find the path that meets the middle, where memory, honesty, and love intersect. Make space for laughter and awkward questions, for retold stories and new ones still developing.

 The aging process has a funny way of tearing down walls and making room for humility, tenderness, and truth, so lean into it and ask the questions, tell the stories, and laugh at the awkward.

Somewhere between the past and the now, hopefully you'll find the real gift of connection.

As you write this shared chapter in real time, consider *actually* writing it. Capture memories like they're expeditions in a travel journal. Chronicle their stories, your reflections, and your bonding journey. Let the memories be for future generations who'll want to know more than just names and dates—they'll really want to know about the escapades of Aunt Rose.

Three
. . .

Advocacy With HIPAA: The Doc Blocker

My dad and stepmother initially lived alone, but as time and aging progressed, my sister moved into the home to offer a higher level of support. She works full time as a flight attendant, so there are still times when the rest of the sibling unit, including myself, have to routinely check in on them. We give each other updates about their day-to-day and everything in between, including the messages that simply say, "I made no progress. Your turn to try."

There's a special kind of endurance test that caregiving never warned us about, which is trying to get a straight answer from your parent after they've attended a doctor's appointment. If you've ever found yourself locked in a conversation loop that feels suspiciously like the old "Who's on First?" baseball skit, congratulations, you've officially entered the professional leagues of parental medical interrogation.

My dad had an appointment for unexplained swelling in his legs and feet, and like any concerned daughter, my sister asked him, "So, what did the doctor say about the swelling?" His response? A casual shrug and a maddening, "Nothing, really." Trying not to jump straight to military DEFCON 1, she inquired, "Well...what did you ask them about it?" He replied, "Oh, I showed them my feet. They just told me to wear compression socks and elevate." Cue to her weighted sigh that probably registered on the Richter scale. She quipped, "Okay, but it's been a week, and I've never seen compression socks anywhere in this house, and you haven't elevated your feet once, unless we count the recliner and the remote." He grinned, completely unbothered, as if her line of questioning was trivia night banter. Meanwhile, she was practically setting up a courtroom reenactment to piece together what exactly had been discussed (and more importantly, what may have been missed) during this mysterious medical visit.

These are the moments when caregiving starts to feel less like managing health and more like solving an unsolvable crime, minus the detective badge, and with way more transitional scenes. You ask questions, and you get riddles to piece together. At the end of it all, you realize that sometimes, loving and caring for aging parents means embracing the absurdity, laughing through the annoyance, and learning to decipher clues like your life, and their circulation, depends on it—all so you can keep going.

When the time feels right, it's important to have a real conversation with your parent about the possibility of having an advocate, whether that's you or someone else they trust to be involved in all medical appointments moving forward. Not to take over their medical decisions or treat them like they can't speak for themselves, but more so putting someone in place who can help remember all the finer details, such as at-home steps, medication routines, and follow-up appointments. Medical appointments move fast, new diagnoses can be overwhelming, and important questions can get lost in the shuffle, so the advocate would be a steady second set of ears and someone to help untangle the often-confusing world of modern healthcare.

We know the adage, "It takes a village." This is the case in any high-need situation. An advocate acts as another layer of protection, ensuring that nothing important gets overlooked and that your parent's voice is fully heard. When framed this way, advocacy becomes an act of partnership and protectiveness, not control and lack of independence. And besides, medical professionals have full teams supporting them—nurses, technicians, pharmacists, office staff, and schedule coordinators—so why shouldn't your parent have someone on their side too?

To help make the conversation about having a trusted loved one become their medical advocate easier, show real-life examples of how advocacy partnerships work close to home. Maybe your friend accompanies her mother to cardiology appointments, takes notes, and asks about new medications so her father doesn't have to feel overwhelmed. Maybe a neighbor's adult son doesn't speak for his father, but he sits quietly through appointments, listens, and asks clarifying questions when needed, making sure nothing gets missed. You can offer to fill that same role to be a partner in care, not a boss. Frame it as teamwork, saying something like,

"You're still the captain of the ship, I'm just here to help read the maps."

Make it clear that it's about making life easier, safer, and less stressful, which would benefit both of you. Knowing they've got a teammate when their health feels fragile or they're just tired of dealing with the *it* can be one of the greatest comforts aging parents experience, even if it takes a little convincing at first.

Now, if you have the conversation with your parents and they agree to make you their advocate, get ready for the next obstacle. If you've ever tried to call a doctor's office for information about a parent's condition only to be hit with a politely firm wall of silence, you've already met The Doc Blocker, also known as HIPAA. The Health Insurance Portability and Accountability Act (HIPAA) is a federal law designed to protect personal health information, ensuring that sensitive medical details aren't shared without explicit permission. In practice, it means that unless your parent fills out the proper paperwork, authorizing you as an approved person, the medical team legally can't share squat, not even to simply find out if your parent showed up for their appointment.

HIPAA isn't meant to frustrate families, but it often does, especially when you're genuinely trying to help. It's not enough to show up with good intentions; advocacy needs to be official. This involves signing HIPAA release forms, naming someone in medical power of attorney paperwork, and ensuring that your parent's doctors, hospitals, and pharmacies have those permissions documented. Without that, you'll find yourself trapped outside the information loop when you're needed most, waving from behind a hazy glass wall of technicalities. So, once your parents agree to make you their advocate (or another trusted loved one), the next conversation will be about signing those papers to allow you to have access to important information. Conversations with your parents around HIPAA might feel heavy, but they're critical to making advocacy functional, not just symbolic. Remind your parent that it's not about giving up privacy; it's about choosing trusted backup when it matters most.

When advocacy is official, it may even be cool to have t-shirts made and wear them to every appointment, such as:

- Yes, I'm with Them. Yes, I Have Questions
- Making Sure "I'm Fine" Gets a Second Opinion
- Primary Advocate. Keeping Doctors on Their Toes
- Healthcare Advocate. No Copay Required

Don't forget the importance of levity, because this process can be wearisome. So, when you're faced with "The Doc Blocker," remember, HIPAA is not your enemy, even when it feels like it, standing on the outside of the information loop. Even if you're the one driving them to appointments, managing their pills, and researching "what is swelling + compression socks + stubbornness," you're still legally considered an outsider unless your parent officially gives permission. The moral of this story is: if you don't have HIPAA paperwork signed, asking the doctor for updates will get you the same answer as asking a Magic 8 Ball: "Ask again later." Be proactive, and work toward getting the forms signed. Turn The Doc Blocker into The Doc Talker.

Now Taking The Mic: Advocating Loudly, Proudly, And With A Giant Binder

One pretty standard Saturday morning, I woke up earlier than usual with the house wrapped in that rare, blissful quiet that feels like winning the lottery of adult life. Naturally, I decided to let everyone sleep, grab some coffee, and steal a few moments of peace before the chaos of my son's baseball game-day prep began. With my cup of caffeine cuddly in hand and optimism in my veins, I even pressed my luck and ran to the grocery store after leaving my husband a text that I'd meet them at the baseball field.

It was shaping up to be a stellar morning until my phone buzzed as I was weighing the impact a box of glazed donuts would have on my hips. It was a text from my husband that casually informed me that my mom had fallen. He assured me that he'd picked her up and tucked her back into bed and that she was only a little shaken. Now, for most people, that kind of text would trigger immediate panic. For me, sadly, it sounded like it was just another minor bump in the road, barely registering above a shrug. After all, she had fallen before, and her falls were usually sub-dramatic slides down the side of the bed or slow-motion stumbles that were more emotionally exhausting than medically urgent. On top of this, I had long learned how to settle in apathy as a protective cape, so in general, my sense of panic was lessened.

Even so, I cut my grocery shopping trip short—but not before I surrendered to the seduction of those weighty donuts—in order to have time to check on my mom. I would pop in to make sure she was okay, then unload the groceries and move on with the preplanned Saturday. However, that plan shattered the moment I walked into her room. Groceries abandoned in the car, I found her lying stiffly in bed, wearing a mask of pain so obvious it practically screamed. When I asked how she felt, she gave me the classic aging parent answer: "I'm fine." That inner thought comic book bubble above my head sarcastically popped up with, "Sure you are."

> *Watching her flinch and grimace just trying to sit up made it clear, this was no regular tuck and roll.*

Within minutes, I was calling 911, and by the time the ambulance doors slammed shut, my "normal Saturday" was a full-blown medical emergency.

Fast forward through exams, X-rays, and the longest emergency department wait of my life, and we learned she had fractured her clavicle and broken her pelvic bone, essentially cutting her already limited mobility down to zero. This was when she was transferred to a nursing facility, and I moved into full-time advocate beast mode.

Every day during that first week, I found myself repeating basic facts about her history, her medication regimen, and her actual pain levels, into a revolving door of staff who treated my mom's chirpy and prideful response of "I'm fine!" as gospel. Meanwhile, I played translator, mind reader, and occasional bad cop to ensure that someone, anyone, dug deeper. And during the moments when I needed to be present at home, my sister ensured that she was with our mom so there was no gap in advocacy. In my absence, she was diligent about getting updates from medical staff and observing their interactions with our mom, which she shared with me so I could stay fully in the loop.

The ongoing "I'm fine" from our mother and the dis-hopeful energy from the medical staff catapulted into after only two weeks, the care team deciding she had "plateaued" and was ready to be discharged in a wheelchair. I was at the meeting with my mother and sister while the care team exclaimed the plateau outcome. This decision came without even bothering to take new X-rays or acknowledging that, medically speaking, her injuries were still mid-heal. I was coated in appalled expressions all over my face, and I recall looking at my sister. She was just as shocked and had an expression of sneering remorse for the care team that seemed to say, "If they didn't really *know* my sister up to this point, they are about to meet her now!"

After the unsettling news of the premature discharge and the silence of the room lingered a bit, I (politely but loudly) pointed out that charting her condition inadequately was practically giving Medicare an easy path to deny her continued care. I added that her return home would place her at further risk and without proper care because she would be home alone for over 10 hours a day due to mine and my husband's work schedules. I asked the team if they had any knowledge of the construct of our home, and of course they didn't, because no one had ever asked. I explained that my home is full of stairs with one flight that is required to get to the kitchen. I strongly explained to them I needed her "care" to be more than a formality.

My wording and tone carried an aura that I would accurately and expediently diminish the facility's 4+ star rating in Yelping heartbeat.

Suddenly, everyone started treating her like she mattered. Funny how that works. I won't pretend I wasn't exhausted, worried sick, and battling the guilty horror of having to eventually leave her alone each evening in a facility that, at the time, I didn't fully trust, but it truly was the better option than having her discharged to go home before she was ready. And in the meantime, my sister and I continued to focus on what we could continue to control and ways we could help by consistently taking turns being alongside our mom during this experience. Above all, we stayed resilient while we fought for exceptional care.

When she was finally discharged two weeks later, a total of 30 days of around-the-clock care, we departed on as equal footing as possible with the care team, having built positive connections forged from persistence and unwavering advocacy. We didn't just leave with discharge papers; we left with at-home support services, a clearer path forward, and a real sense of optimism that my mother would heal stronger and more independent than before. As for my mom, she left standing with a quad cane in one hand and an earned sense of accomplishment and sentiments of truly feeling cared for by facility staff.

I share this story to highlight the struggle and how hard it can be to advocate. It didn't feel comfortable for me to step outside of my normal demeanor to persist pointedly at medical professionals, but my advocacy was fueled from caring about my mom's level of care and pushing back when the use of "care" was an evident formality as opposed to a sincere reality. Whether it's speaking with hospital staff or a doctor during a routine appointment, communication and general attentiveness during these moments are essential, and I'm not just talking about the pleasantries at the beginning of an appointment. It's about developing a strong, collaborative relationship with your parent's healthcare team so you get comfortable asking the tough questions and become familiar enough that they slow down and listen to your concerns. With this approach, you'll be on your way to becoming a well-informed, assertive advocate. Think of it as your superpower, the power of effective communication in the face of awful bedside manner and medical obscurities.

However, when flexing your superpower, don't underestimate the power of preparation. Think of this as your pregame ritual, your mental stretching before entering the medical advocacy arena. Before any appointment, gather all relevant information: your parent's medical history (including previous diagnoses, medications, allergies, and surgical procedures), recent test results, and a list of your questions and observations. This is especially helpful if your parent isn't part of a Health Maintenance Organization (HMO) insurance system of care. HMOs typically have an all-encompassing system of records that most all doctors in the HMO have access to, while the Preferred Provider Organization (PPO) insurance system of care doesn't always.

In the case of PPOs, some medical care is not centralized or united from one office to another, so it requires patients to be forthcoming, able, and willing to provide medical history information to the professionals. For example, with a PPO, the primary care doctor can approve a referral to a podiatrist that has a different office and medical file. The file could be absent of things, such as allergies to medication or if the patient already has a current prescription for a particular medication. I've found it incredibly helpful to keep a dedicated folder with pertinent information neatly organized. Keep in mind that digital isn't always foolproof because power outages and computer crashes do happen, so I recommend having a physical copy as well.

Writing down your questions about your parent's care is imperative. Vague questions lead to vague answers, and since we need precise, concrete information to make informed decisions, I recommend avoiding the question, "Is my mom, okay?" Instead, try, "Dr. Smith, could you explain the results of the recent MRI, specifically what the findings in the lumbar region indicate?" Or, "Can you please explain the diagnosis of congestive heart failure in a way I can understand?" Or, "What are the potential side effects of this medication, and how likely are they to occur?" The level of detail will improve the quality of the response significantly. The more specific you are, the better equipped the doctor is to address your concerns directly and effectively since they know exactly what you're asking.

During the appointment, don't be afraid to interrupt (tactfully, of course). If something is unclear, stop the conversation and ask for clarification. Many doctors appreciate patients who actively participate in their care. When looking at the opposite end of this, passively accepting whatever information is given, I've heard responses from people such as, "Well, the doctor didn't tell me, so it must not be important." Please, don't get trapped in this cycle of insanity. It's important to understand that medical professionals may wear the white coat, but they are still human, they have family matters and disruptions like everyone else, and they, too, are capable of having lapses or misreading the room. So, ask questions, even if you think they may be ridiculous, and most likely they won't be. And if the doctor makes you feel like they are, or if you don't feel that their answers are sufficient or taken into genuine consideration, don't be afraid to seek a second opinion. The first doctor you see may not be the right fit, and that's okay.

Building bridges with all healthcare providers (nurses, physician assistants, pharmacists, technicians, schedulers, therapists, social workers, etc.) is about mutual respect and understanding. Each professional has a specialized understanding that they can use to supplement your treatment plan and to resolve problems quickly. Of course, you aren't becoming a doctor yourself (unless that online anatomy course finally calls your name), but move like you're on the same team, working toward a common goal. Because you are!

 You're not their adversary; you're their partner in caring for your parent.

Treat them respectfully, articulate your concerns clearly, and don't be afraid to ask questions or take notes. This proactive approach could create a more positive experience for all involved.

Pills, Drills, And Calendar Thrills

You're not exactly sure when it happened. The day you reached for the cinnamon to spice up some toast, and the next thing you knew, the spice cabinet had quietly transformed into a rogue pharmacy. The paprika has been pushed aside, the bay leaves replaced by prescription bottles, and shelves sag under the weight of medications with names longer than most German cities. You see duplicate prescriptions from different doctors, "get better quick" vitamins bought during an infomercial spree, expired medications clinging to relevance, and pills that, according to late-night online research, absolutely should not be mingling at the same dinner party. "What are all these medications for?" you ask your parent, but all you get is a lengthy ponder followed by a confident, "They're for my heart...and my legs...and maybe my thyroid?" The truth is, memory recall changes as we age, and managing a complicated list of medications without a clear system is a risky game of chance. Without updated medication lists, without clear diagnoses documented and ready, every new doctor's visit becomes a guessing game, where losing means hospital visits, medication reactions, or worse.

>
> *And if you have two aging parents in the same house, congratulations, you've unlocked the boss level kerfuffle of medication management.*

That cabinet now multiplies in horror: two blood pressure medications here, three cholesterol medications there, a few mystery pills that might actually be just Tic Tacs. It's a terrifying carnival of pill bottles, and let's not even get started again on the PPO system of care maze. Veterans Affairs on one side, private and public insurance on the other, none of the systems talking to each other. So, one doctor prescribes something, and then another doctor prescribes something else, and guess who is left holding the bag of confusion. At least rival sports teams keep score. You develop a growing sense of dread every time someone says "referral" or "prescription" because without active oversight, nobody's connecting the dots on drug interactions, redundant medications, or outdated prescriptions. It becomes painfully clear: no one is quarterbacking this but you, and by the time someone notices something's wrong, it's usually very wrong.

This is where the drills part of "Pills, Drills, and Calendar Thrills" comes in. Make it a non-negotiable practice to bring an updated medication list to every doctor's appointment. Present the list to the doctor even if it isn't asked for (they will probably thank you later). Also, make sure there are enough refills ordered, and check in with the doctor to reconfirm that all the medications remain appropriate. Label everything clearly at home; use a giant plastic bag if you must, whatever it takes to keep medications organized and easy to review at a moment's notice.

However, keep in mind, even with a solid plan and organization regarding the medication, the system can still come with challenges—things can change often, or your parents can make a mistake, either taking more or less than prescribed. If your parent is struggling to take their prescriptions as directed, regardless of how well they're organized, it's a clear sign that their health and well-being could be at risk. One of the most caring steps you can take is to offer to lift that responsibility from their shoulders. Present it as an act of teamwork, letting them know how much you appreciate the care they've given you over the years. Proudly share that you want to return the favor with gratitude by taking over their medication schedule, ensuring they're supported and safe.

If you aren't quite at the point of taking over the medication regimen, it would still be a good idea to regularly check the pill organizer to ensure that your parent is taking their medications as prescribed. Subtle clues can signal potential problems, such as an unusually large number of pills left over or missing. If this happens, don't dismiss it as inconsequential. These clues could indicate a more significant problem, such as forgetfulness, confusion, or even a deliberate refusal to take the medication.

If you've identified these problems, address them with your parent, specifically with the goal of now taking your regular medication checks a step further by having a hand in the actual dosing. For example, if your parent has routinely forgotten to take medication, you might say, "Would it be helpful if we set a reminder on your phone so you don't have to keep everything in your head? Even I'd forget, with all these pills." Or if you're concerned about your parent's refusal to take the medication, you might start by saying, "I've been wondering if any of these meds are making you feel off. What do you think about us talking to the doctor together to see if anything needs a tweak?"

Having a regular drill of monitoring your parent's overall health goes beyond just managing medications.

It involves being observant, proactive, and, yes, sometimes a bit nosy.

Gain knowledge on how to regularly check your parent's vital signs, what to look for, and what methods to use, such as when checking their blood pressure, heart rate, and temperature, for example. Many devices are available to aid in this process, ranging from simple home blood pressure monitors to more advanced devices. Consult with your parent's doctor to determine how to accurately monitor their vitals, when monitoring results deem it necessary to bring to their attention, and how often monitoring should occur.

Finally, those calendar thrills, because no medication management system is complete without one. You're not just juggling pill times; you're juggling specialist appointments, lab work deadlines, insurance authorization windows, and prescription refill timing. A solid calendar—paper, digital, or dry-erase board—becomes your lifeline. Set reminders and color-code them for medications, appointments, and tasks, if that helps. Write everything down, and assume, for example, that if a follow up appointment is not on the calendar, it doesn't exist. Because by Tuesday, you too will forget if that blood work was at 8:30 or 10:15, and your future sanity will thank you (Hell! You're getting old, too). Organizing pills, planning doctor visits, and managing health is not sexy or glamorous work. It's hardly ever found in a highlight reel, but it's the foundation that keeps your parent safe, stable, and thriving at the end of the day.

Four

...

Namaste...Over There: Accepting Imperfection

PREPARING TO HEAD BACK TO WORK AFTER A 30-DAY CAREGIVING leave to care for my mom after her discharge from the nursing home, my body was bouncing between a foggy emotional hangover and a determination to regain some normalcy. Mind you, during my caregiving leave, I rarely had a chance to elevate pride in my appearance, which was unusual for me. Being able to reintegrate into a world outside of full-time household management, therapy updates, and coordinating in-home visits was as invigorating as it was daunting.

That morning, I launched into my routine like a woman possessed. I managed everyone's wake-ups, reviewed food prep and medication regimens, interacted with and fed the puppy, and whirled through the remaining kitchen chaos. Finally, I was able to turn my attention to myself, triple-checking everything.

I made sure I had my three essential bags: my work tote, snack pack, and my emotional baggage.

I zipped out of the house on time and dressed, feeling victorious. As I neared work and casually glanced at my rearview mirror, my victory plummeted to dreadful defeat. There they were, sitting proudly atop my head: my hot pink, leopard print foam rollers attached tightly to my braided hair.

Time was of the essence, and I was nearly in the parking lot. There was no turning back. I stared at myself, wide-eyed, wondering if I could somehow summon my edge control hair gel, brush, comb, or the power of invisibility. But, of course, no such luck. So, after parking, I snatched each roller from my head, and I did what any mildly unraveling woman would do—I stealthily hurried inside and hoped my self-awareness would outrun the surprise of seeing me mixed with confused looks. Now, on the way to my desk, I did a mental recall, wondering if I even brushed my teeth and put on deodorant.

Absentmindedly, I bumped into a friend, who took one look at me with a compassionate grin in that way only a battle-weary working woman could, and said, "Girl, it's okay. Just go namaste over there and take your time doing your hair." I did exactly what she suggested, but only after a big exhale, uncontrollable laugh, and tear-tinged eyes that weren't from shame but from being supported and the sheer relief of being able to laugh at myself.

Sometimes we just need to look at ourselves with a newfound focus, like making a bold move to take back that "straw that broke the camel's back," kick our feet up, and pick the grit (shame, lack of self-compassion, the expectation of others, etc.) from our teeth with it. Self-compassion doesn't always look like a spa day or being transfixed within the comfort of a sound bath. It sometimes looks like simply forgiving yourself for the uninvited foam rollers, a missed commitment, and the slow unraveling of your last shred of sexy.

That morning arriving at work, I was hit with a wave of dread, and then something that offered brightness: a friend and a "well, this is where I'm at" body-buckling laugh. In that brief, unscripted moment, I was reminded that grace shows up best when pride takes a nap.

> *The reality is, we're doing a thousand things at once—feeding, planning, working, caregiving—and something will absolutely fall through the cracks.*

That day, it was my hair, and tomorrow, it might be forgetting to wash my son's school P.E. clothes or thaw chicken for dinner. I won't pretend this level of grace within ourselves is easy, but I try to make a consistent effort to leave space for my humanity just so that I can breathe. My stance is, if the world doesn't implode when we show up dusty and undone, maybe that's permission to be gentler with ourselves.

Self-compassion in specific regard to caregiving isn't a grand announcement, either. It's a private agreement with yourself that "trying" has merit and accepting that not every day will be sophisticated. Sometimes, caregiving means being fully devoted and understanding that you probably missed something. It means resenting the mental overload and mourning the loss of your personal time, but still knowing this doesn't change how deeply you love your parents. I've tried to focus on catching myself pre- or mid-spiral by saying, "Okay, let's try that again." We hold ourselves to unreachable standards with no pregame warm-up and then wonder why we're exhausted.

Forgiving ourselves for not being superhuman every day is the most thoughtful gift we can give to our tired, over-worked selves.

 It is not weakness; it's vulnerable survival with soul.

You deserve your own understanding because you will forget things, and you will lose your cool. You will find lip balm in your bra, your wallet in the freezer, and forget why you walked into a room. You will also love fiercely, show up relentlessly, and grow in ways you didn't ask for but now carry like a noteworthy tattoo. Frankly, this chapter of life is demanding and unscripted, but within those moments are proof that you're doing the best you can and with the energy you've got. And on days when you fall short, you don't need inner or outer criticism. You need grace, a laugh, and maybe a friend who whispers, "Namaste over there, boo. You're doing just fine."

It's Not Selfish, It's Survival. Now Hand Me The Moisturizer!

The importance of self-care has been mentioned a couple of times already, but we're here again because that's how important it is! Self-care isn't selfish; it's the deliberate move to maintain and enhance self-preservation. You cannot run a household, raise kids, hold down a career, coordinate appointments, stay on top of medication refills, field insurance calls, and be expected to perform optimally through it all just because someone labeled you as strong.

 You are not invincible; you are a whole person with limits, feelings, and needs.

That image of showing up to work with foam rollers in my hair—it wasn't just funny, it was symbolic. That's what happens when you don't hit pause. You get reminders from your reflection in the mirror, your calendar, your tone, and your blood pressure (if you've even checked it lately) that something has to give while still showing yourself compassion that you didn't notice sooner. What needs to give is the guilt around needing rest, space, or a few minutes to have your own thoughts. Self-care is about protecting the person who, routinely and without needed applause, makes everything else function: you.

When it comes to taking time for yourself, people aren't going to just give you space. You have to take it like you want it. That means putting others on notice with loving and well-defined boundaries. When you are faced with needing space for yourself, try telling your crew,

 "Between 7:00 and 7:30, I'm not available unless someone is bleeding, or Beyoncé is at the door."

Yes, it might only be 30 minutes in the bathroom with a face mask and an audiobook, but it's your 30 minutes. To those that really want to help but don't know how, an occasional spa or coffee gift card or even an expression of appreciation will land pretty well.

If you feel a need to provide more of an explanation, set the tone with statements like, "I'm recharging so I can show up better for everyone," or if you'd prefer to keep it simple, you can keep it at the more direct version: "No, I'm not available right now." If there's any pushback, you can then ask, "If I burn out, what's plan B?" Or, "If I don't take care of myself, everything we've built together may start falling apart. I'm trying not to let that happen. Does that sound fair?" It's not over-indulgence; that's you understanding your relevance and commitment to yourself and others.

I believe self-care comes in levels, and they all count, so don't discount the small, segmented little rituals that rebuild and recharge you. I began to implement many levels of self-care. On the "bare minimum but still winning" end, it could mean sitting in my car alone with the seat reclined for 15 minutes before walking into the house, lying in my hammock, or secretly eating my own snacks without sharing.

My medium-level self-care might look like taking a break from people who drain my energy, lighting a candle, and drinking something warm in a quiet corner, or finally scheduling that physical I've been putting off for too long so the weight of the task is off my shoulders.

My high-tier self-care may be a weekend away, a solo movie date, a little "just for me" shopping, or my "I'm taking a full Saturday off and nobody better bother me unless it's someone handling me coffee, carbs, and compliments simultaneously or someone holding a million-dollar Publishers Clearing House cardboard check." These short, intentional pauses give me a momentary escape from the relentless pace of caregiving, career, and life. Even in those brief windows, I find clarity, focus, and surprisingly, a lighter mood. This time gives me permission to process the absurd, confront the emotions I keep shelving, and to make sense of the small, powerful moments that often go unnoticed.

Sometimes when you start prioritizing yourself, you might ruffle a few feathers; that's okay, as long as you're communicating. New things tend to disrupt old patterns and build growth. You've probably trained the people around you to see you as the "go-to." It could be a hard realization, but much of the demands placed upon us, we've allowed to happen. By demonstrating that you deserve care too, you're modeling something healthy for everyone who's watching you navigate this caregiving life. That includes your kids, your aging parents, your partner, and yourself five years from now. Choosing yourself is never the wrong choice, especially when some days, your peace has been taxed harder than your paycheck.

Hustling, Healing, And Hoping For The Best

Caring for aging parents isn't a manual-driven, curated guide handed down through generations. It's a chaotic, weather-raging road trip in a car with one working windshield wiper, a disoriented navigation system, and everyone in the back yelling different directions. However, through the fog of fall alarms, the aroma of bodily existence, repeated stories, endearing memories, forgotten appointments, and miraculous rebounds, you've shown up. You've somehow managed to hustle through doctor's visits and grocery store runs, advocate like a trial lawyer, love like a poet, and still remember to pick up dog food on the way home. That deserves more than praise—it deserves peace, snacks, and a really solid nap.

If self-care still sounds more like a fantasy, it may become easier to embrace when you adjust your perspective; deeper than the exhaustion and the punchlines, there's something sacred about what you're doing, and *that* deserves self-compassion.

> *There is healing in this complex, beautiful labor of care (even though an epidural would've been nice).*

There is hope tucked inside each moment of clarity, every shared laugh, every "remember when" that surfaces unexpectedly while folding laundry or watching game shows together. You are building a legacy, not just of obligation, but of devotion. And yes, the way you care now might just be the blueprint your own children pull out one day when you start arguing with the TV remote or swearing that you already took your medication (even though you didn't). Absorb this possibility; let that thought sit with you a minute. What you're doing today isn't invisible, it's planting seeds of compassion, humanity, and affection. While you may not get a trophy or a parade in your name, trust that this sacred hustle will echo forward in ways you can't even see yet.

> *Keep pushing on with grace when you have it, grit when you don't, and humor always.*

There will be better days, lighter loads, and sweeter memories ahead. When in doubt, take the break, take a walk, and eat the snack. While not everyone is on this ride yet, soon, and possibly unexpectedly, most will be handed a metaphorical ticket and told, "You're up." So, to the reader, wherever you are in the journey of prepping, withstanding, recovering, I acknowledge your labor, your late-night worry, your whispered prayers, and your tight smile when in advocacy beast mode. Remind yourself that you're not just surviving caregiving, you're shaping it into something powerful, something generous, and something beautifully unforgettable. This work you do (or will do) is heavy, but it matters and will be meaningful for future generations.

With much love and well wishes,

—Shannon

Acknowledgments
. . .

To my parents, the ones who carried me in their arms, the ones who grasped me on their laps in car rides, the ones who balanced me on their shoulders so I could see the world when my curiosity thrived, and now occasionally allow me to pluck at their nerves: thank you for your love, your sacrifices, and for teaching me how to show up and show stop. Helping you navigate the colorful kaleidoscope of aging can be challenging, haphazardly hazy, and sometimes exasperatingly full of next-level adulting negotiations, but no matter the interwoven platform we stand on in these moments, I carry deep gratitude for the sacrifices, lessons, and love that shaped me into who I am today. It is with the utmost honor that I now walk beside you, giving back through love, service, and unwavering support.

To my husband, thank you for being the emotional crash pad when I showed up with my patience threadbare and my energy evaporated. You caught more of my sighs, rolled eyes, and caffeine-deprived rants than anyone should reasonably endure; yet you kept me steady.

To my siblings, thank you for giving what you can, when you can. Every effort matters, even if it doesn't show up in a perfectly timed group text.

To my tribe of friends in the caregiving trenches, your stories, your heartfelt confessions, and occasional "what the hell!" texts remind me that I'm not alone walking the tightrope between duty and meltdown.

To my editor, thank you for lending me your keen eye and steady guidance throughout this process. Your care, passion for the topic, and insightful suggestions helped me transform my book into what I truly wanted it to be.

Finally, to my children, thank you for allowing me to carve out time for this book, even when it stole a little from our everyday moments. And thank you in advance for the days when you'll help guide me with the same mix of humor and love that's gotten us this far. I hope your future caregiving stories are worth retelling—I promise to make my aging at least *somewhat* entertaining.

Resource Roundup

. . .

THE RESOURCES BELOW OFFER EVERYTHING FROM LOCAL SUPPORT services and practical caregiving tips to emotional guidance and connection. If you've reached a point where you feel overwhelmed, please know there's no shame in needing help, only strength in asking for it. You don't have to do this alone, and with the right support, it really can become more manageable and even meaningful. Hope and help do exist, and you deserve both.

Eldercare Locator: www.eldercare.acl.gov

Eldercare Locator is a nationwide service that connects older adults and caregivers with trustworthy local support resources. It helps with finding services like transportation, home care, housing, and legal aid based on your zip code.

AARP Family Caregiving Resources: www.aarp.org/caregiving

AARP Family Caregiving offers comprehensive information and tools for adults caring for aging parents, spouses, or loved ones. They provide help with navigating healthcare, legal planning, financial decisions, and emotional support for caregivers at any stage.

National Alliance for Caregiving: www.caregiving.org

National Alliance for Caregiving is a nonprofit coalition focused on supporting and advocating for family caregivers across the U.S. It helps with research, policy development, and sharing best practices to improve the caregiver experience.

The National Resource Center for Engaging Older Adults: www.usaging.org

This center is designed to support professional and organizations working to increase meaningful engagement opportunities for older adults. It offers guidance on combating social isolation and promoting volunteerism, community connection, and lifelong learning.

National Institute on Aging: www.nia.nih.gov

The National Institute on Aging is a government research institute dedicated to the health and well-being of older adults. It offers evidence-based information on aging, Alzheimer's disease, caregiving, and healthy lifestyle choices.

Medicare: www.medicare.gov

Medicare is a federal health insurance program primarily for people aged 65 and older, as well as some younger individuals with disabilities. It helps cover hospital stays, doctor visits, prescription drugs, and other essential medical services.

Medicaid: www.medicaid.gov

Medicaid is a joint federal and state program that provides health coverage to eligible low-income individuals and families, such as older adults, people with disabilities, children, and pregnant women. It helps with long-term care services, home healthcare, and medical costs not covered by Medicare, especially for those needing financial assistance for medical care.

Meals on Wheels America: www.mealsonwheelsamerica.org

Meals on Wheels America is a national nonprofit organization that provides resources to community-based programs to support older adults across the United States. Their mission is to improve the health and quality of life of seniors by providing nutritious meals, friendly visits, and wellness checks to ensure that no one is left hungry or isolated.

The U.S. Department of Veterans Affairs: www.va.gov

The U.S. Department of Veterans Affairs provides benefits and services for veterans, their families, and survivors. It helps with healthcare, financial assistance, caregiver support programs, and long-term care resources for aging veterans.

Social Security Administration (SSA): www.ssa.gov

The SSA is a federal agency responsible for managing Social Security benefits for retirees, people with disabilities, and surviving family members. It helps with income support, Medicare enrollment, and retirement planning guidance.

About The Author

. . .

SHANNON WEST IS A STORYTELLER and a compassionate caregiver to her parents who humbly strives to navigate the intricate dance of all the layers of life. A seasoned professional mentor, she maintains a meticulous, organized schedule and a talent of keeping a steadfast cheerfulness and perspective. Her life is a vibrant tapestry woven from family responsibilities, professional ambitions, inspirational pursuits, and the demanding role of caregiver, all fueled by copious amounts of coffee.

This debut book, *Caring for Aging Parents Without Losing Your Mind!*, is a mere prelude to a rich literary legacy and is a poignant testament to profound experiences supporting aging parents. It's a heartfelt narrative infused with humor, empathy, and pragmatic advice, forged in the crucible of chaotic caregiving, seasoned with unflinching advocacy.

Beyond the challenges of personal life, Shannon dedicates herself to public service, empowering individuals entangled within the justice system. In her leisure time, she finds solace and inspiration in writing, the thrill of sporting events, the quiet escape of reading, and the rewarding work of guiding others toward professional excellence through mentorship and consultation.

www.ingramcontent.com/pod-product-compliance
Lightning Source LLC
LaVergne TN
LVHW061555070526
838199LV00077B/7051